The Almighty Mackerel
and
His Holy Bootstraps

Waking Up To Who You Really Are

J.C. Amberchele

NON-DUALITY PRESS

THE ALMIGHTY MACKEREL AND HIS HOLY BOOTSTRAPS

First edition published March 2011 by NON-DUALITY PRESS

© J.C. Amberchele 2011
© Non-Duality Press 2011

Cover image from a tapestry entitled *Presencia de la Diosa del Agua*
by Máximo Laura (www.maximolaura.com)
Photograph by Humberto Valdivia

NON-DUALITY PRESS | PO Box 2228 | Salisbury | SP2 2GZ
United Kingdom

ISBN: 978-0-9566432-4-7

www.non-dualitypress.com

The Almighty Mackerel
and
His Holy Bootstraps

Contents

Introduction ix
Foreword xi

PART I

Truth 3
Self-Improvement 5
Choice 9
Experience 12
Source, No-Source 15
Whatever You Say 17
Know Thyself 19
Seeing 21
Ding-Dong 23
Heaven And Hell 26
God Incarnate 28
Calvary 31
Blink: Revelation And Salvation 33
Within 34
Gratitude 36

PART II

Pie In The Sky.. 41
The Greatest Show On Earth 45
No Credentials..49
Gifts 53
Pleased To Meet Me...56
Loss..61
A Matter Of Life And Death 64

The Almighty Mackerel 69
Upside Down And Backwards 72
Compassion 77
Truth Is Simply Truth 80
The Kingdom Of Heaven 83
Clear As Mud 86
The Great Fool..92
Not An Option 97
Space And Time 102
Control 108
The Whole Enchilada 114
The One Thought 116
Fulfillment 119
Shadow Boxing 121
Everything Matters 124
To Meditate Or Not To Meditate 133
The New Religion 135
Seeing One, Seeing All 140
Reincarnation Revisited 142
Friends 149
Divine Work 153
Solipsism 156
Will 161
Responsibility 167
What You See Is What You Get 170
What Is, Is 173
Suffering 176
God Wears Many Disguises 180
Re-Appearance 185
It's Called Freedom 188
The Hamster Wheel 191
The Grand Scheme Of Things 193
Ed The Talking Horse 198
Everywhere, There's Music 201
Vanity 206
His Holy Bootstraps 209

Rational Mind, Desperate Souls 212
The Ten-Gallon Hat 217
Scam Artist 221

INTRODUCTION

Perhaps if something is said over and over a hundred different ways, it will finally sink in. And perhaps not. But if it is *seen* just once....

This book is an offering by the Absolute; an expression of a realization ultimately had by no one. Part I is comprised of 15 essays. The dialogues in Part II are based on conversations with five other incarcerated men over a period of four years. The author is indebted to these men, and to the English philosopher and spiritual teacher Douglas E. Harding for the awareness exercises and many of the terms presented in this book, and for his unique and incomparable expression of non-dual wisdom.

May these essays and dialogues lead you to the center of your being, the only Being there is. They are, in the final sense, messages from you to you.

FOREWORD

One reason why awakening is so difficult to share is that, because it is so easy to see, nobody believes it. Another reason is that it is so devastating to the ego, so threatening to the idea that one is a separate self, that it is deeply feared. Those who say that awakening requires great struggle and many years or lifetimes to achieve are those who aren't ready for it, who prefer to remain a separate self, a seeker on the path to enlightenment.

And that is as it should be. Ego consciousness appears as a necessary step on the road to egoless awakening, for how could ultimate absence be seen here if there were no presence imagined there? And after all, ego consciousness is not a mistake, for who is there separate to dream it up? Who other than What You Are – the Totality – dreams anything up?

Then why do anything? Why strive to awaken when even the lack of awakening is What You Are? The answer, of course, is that there is no one separate from What You Are to exercise the choice. The impetus arises from No-thing and appears within the All, and in the case of this particular self, it appeared as an unquenchable thirst in several forms:

First and foremost, I wanted respite from my past – anything that would relieve the shame of a life dedicated to selfish pursuits at the expense of others. I knew that the answer would have to be radical, as radical as death itself, for nothing I had previously read or been told or practiced in the areas of psychology or philosophy or religion had had any meaningful effect. The burden of being who I thought I was was just too heavy.

But I had once had a glimpse of the freedom I was seeking during several LSD sessions in the 1960s, and I knew that the answer lay within. And after viewing a Joseph Campbell series on PBS in the 1980s, the quest began in earnest to re-discover that sense of freedom and how I could capture it and hold onto it and solve the problem of my life. Guided mostly by intuition, I began reading anything that seemed related to my LSD experiences, namely the wisdom teachings of the great sages of India and Tibet and China, as well as the Christian and Sufi mystics. Mostly I wanted confirmation of what I had momentarily seen and somehow knew to be true – although I couldn't say what that was. The search was on, and it was relentless. It was as if I had boarded a train I couldn't get off.

And there was ego gratification in this search. I was now on the Great Path, a true seeker/follower, involved in something more meaningful and more important, I figured, than the efforts of any corporate CEO or Head of State. This was the Big Question, the Holy Grail, and I was hot on the trail of it. What better reason to continue?

But below the surface there continued an impossible and confusing longing for someone or something to fill what felt like a gaping hole in my chest, appearing and reappearing on the surface as a crippling sense of worthlessness and loneliness. I was writhing inside with a lack that not even the identity of a spiritual seeker could fill.

There was also the question of life and death and spending the rest of the former in prison. I was convinced I had wasted my life thus far, and I was compelled to no longer do so. There was the matter of presence – I was present, I was here, I had been born into this world and was still alive, and I wanted to know in the time I had left just what this "life" really was, what "I" was, beyond my name, my past, or what others saw or called me. I couldn't imagine how others could seemingly spend their entire lives without wondering why they were or what this universe was that they supposedly found themselves in. How did this happen, how did I happen, and why was I aware? What was awareness?

There was also the abiding sense of being "different." I wasn't satisfied with the explanations of others, not of religious leaders or scientists or even the sages I admired. I wanted to know, to experience for myself what the Great Ones were talking about, this mystery that lay at the heart of the world's wisdom teachings. I wanted to know it, not know about it, and I approached whatever was said with caution, with doubt.

And the more I read, the more I was told that I wasn't who I thought I was, that the world wasn't what it seemed, and, moreover, that I, as who I really was – this Presence I felt – was none other than the center and the source of the universe! The message was certainly radical enough, and if it was true, it just might mean that I would discover the answer to my questions, not to mention the solution to my woes. But was it true? How would I ever know for sure?

And then one day, after years on the search, I read an article by a man who told me to point at where I thought I had a face and look at what I was looking out of – and instantly all of the questions were wordlessly answered. I *saw*, actually saw, what I was, and *knew* what all the sages had been talking about – it was so plainly obvious, so totally available, so Here, and there wasn't the slightest doubt as to Who it was, Who *I* was. And I was no-thing: void, empty, wide awake, boundless, and nothing at all like I thought I was. Here, who I thought I was was gone, replaced by the scene. Gone as a separate self, and one-hundred-percent present as Presence Itself.

And yet to this day the separate self remains, like a favorite robe, slipping comfortably on and off, seemingly of its own accord. This all-too-human idea, astonishing in its complexity and power, although no longer central, no longer believed or identified with, like an intimate and loyal friend, is found to be *inside* of Who I Am, inside of this Awake No-thing, along with everything else it is interdependently linked to, which is the universe itself.

And remarkably the impetus continues. No longer a quest, the destination now revealed as the beginning, still it unfolds, delights in its enthusiasm and endless disguises, dances and laughs with itself, knows itself as the Mystery of Mysteries, and in that unknowing is both surprised and content.

PART 1

TRUTH

There are truths and there are untruths, and there are a myriad of renditions and gradations of each. And then there is Truth. Truth has no opposite. There are no different versions, no degrees or shades of Truth. Truth be told, truth cannot be told. Thus it is said to he unsayable, spoken of as unspeakable, described as indescribable, for it is no-thing, is void, empty, absent even of absence – and for this reason is Presence Itself.

Truth is timeless. It has no beginning or end. Therefore the way and the goal are the same, and that way and that goal is Looking To See. All the religions of the world fall short of Truth because Truth is not religious. Everything that has ever been said in the name of God or Buddha or Self can be discarded in favor of one look. For only Looking To See will open the gate to Truth.

The proposition is that at the very center of your being lies Truth. That which you think is "your being" is not "yours" but is Truth Itself. You have no separate being apart from Truth. You as who you think you are have nothing to do with it, nothing to do with anything except as Truth having everything to do with Itself.

Because Truth is at the center of your being, it is easy to see. But like a man peering through his glasses searching for his glasses, it is so easy to see that you miss it. In fact, Truth is what you are, where you are, when you are. It is never anywhere or any when else because there is not anywhere or any when that you are not. Truth is everything that you see, hear, touch, taste, think, or feel because there is nothing outside of what you are. Truth is Who You Are, seeing only Yourself, and you are both the seer and the seen – simply said, you are Seeing Itself.

Thus the directive is to look. Look back. Look at what is looking. Turn your attention 180 degrees from where you normally look "out there" and see the awake emptiness here where you are. Notice that it has no edges, no boundaries, is infinite in scope; is pure, clear, transparent emptiness, and for that reason is open capacity for the world, is luminous space wedded to what fills it, always right here, always nearer than anything because everything fits within it.

This seeing who you are is not mysterious or vague or somehow veiled. On the contrary, it is simple, concrete, available. Likewise, it is revealed in simple, childlike ways, ways that might seem ridiculous or naive to those of us who value what we have learned and who we have become.

To anyone steeped in objective thinking, the sage may seem a simpleton, a fool, especially when that sage lifts his hand and points an index finger at his face and tells us he sees he is the source of the universe, that in place of a head he has the world, that should we bother to check in like manner, perhaps we would discover the same.

For Truth cannot be reached by intellectual understanding. Talking and reading about Truth is not the same as seeing Truth. Words can become a barrier and, far too often, an escape from the realization of Who You Are. But for seekers of Truth, however many paths are taken, the arrival is a single step through the eye of a needle, and that step is not a word but a look, is not outward but inward. And what does one see here? Surely not the eye of a needle but an Eye as vast as the cosmos, an Eye that holds and beholds all that one is – the universe itself. Look, and see for yourself!

-

SELF-IMPROVEMENT

Forget trying to change yourself (as if you could forget that!).
Drop the idea of improving your situation (as if you could
drop it!). Let it go (as if you could let it go!), because it will
never happen to who you think you are by who you think
you are. Who you think you are is a regional appearance,
and a regional appearance cannot move or act on its own any
more than a shadow can. That separate self, that individual
person you think you are is an objective manifestation of
this Pure Subjectivity, and as such is one among an endless
number of manifestations conditioned by an infinite array of
interconnected forces and events.

But change is the reason you became a spiritual seeker,
you say. Having tried everything else – money, sex, alcohol,
drugs, sports, shopping, television, video games, marriage,
family, therapy, religion – and finding no relief from the
angst, the fear of being trapped, of being imprisoned in a
body, of being helpless, powerless, inconsequential in the
face of the unimaginable vastness of the universe, of never
being free from the feeling that something is missing, you
have come to the mystics and seers for the answer, for the
bliss and fulfillment they offer.

And yet you are aware that suffering is part of being
human. This is what it is like to be a regional appearance,
one among many. Being in the world, a human being is a victim of circumstances – good or bad, peaceful or terrifying,
abundant or hopeless. It is the nature of a "thing" in a world
of things to arise, to suffer experience, and to pass away.
This is what being human is all about: joy, beauty, pain, loss,
triumph, defeat. It is *lila*, the play of *maya*, the great dream
we dream and believe to be all there is.

But it isn't all there is. The dream character you think you are is not who you really are; it is only one of your appearances, while you are so much less and so much more. In fact, you are all the way less, better said as *No-thing*, and all the way more, better said as *Everything*, and all that lies between.

And you would settle for halfway measures, for the comparatively paltry human experiences of bliss and fulfillment, as if that were the real goal, as if that were God. Why not go for the granddaddy of all improvements, which is the perfection of Who You Really Are? Because Who You Really Are, right now, is perfection itself!

And this is the answer to the question of self-improvement: that, for whatever reason, call it grace or divine intervention, you finally decide to look and see and be This Which You Are. As Jesus of Nazareth is said to have said, "Seek ye first the Kingdom of Heaven, and the rest shall be added unto thee."

Because you cannot improve your*self* and then become enlightened. You don't perfect the appearance you identify with and reach a state of Buddhamind or union with God. There is no "becoming" awake, because you are Awakeness Itself. So the apparent improvements you seek as a separate self, if they come at all, come as a *result* of seeing and being who you already are. And come to *all* of your levels of appearance, quarks to galaxies. In the light of the divine Awareness that you are, all are beneficiaries: atoms, molecules, cells, humanity, life, earth, stars – your true "body," which is the universe. All "beings" are enlightened when you see the Light, because all beings are inside of the One Luminous Awareness that you are, and therefore *are* you.

And what might be some of these improvements? What might show up at the level of your*self*, body and mind? Bathed in the awareness of Pure Subjectivity, your atoms, molecules, cells and organs may experience less stress, more harmony, and you may notice lower blood pressure and heart rate, fewer colds and flu, the absence of heart disease or cancer in your life, or even the reversal of such diseases that are already in place. You may live longer – and do so with more energy, with less ego drama; not having to put up a front, worrying less (or not at all) about what others think, or even about what *you* think, psychic and physical energy is allowed to flow unimpeded from you, its Source.

You may be inspired more. You may be more creative. No longer trapped in a mind and body, you may use your mind and body as it can best be used, meeting each situation with openness and equanimity and the propensity to solve problems rather than create them or complain about them.

You may enjoy life more, savor the world in all its sublime variety, even discover the difficult times to be sought-after adventures. No longer seeing yourself as a tiny speck in a vast and unforgiving universe but rather as the all-encompassing Capacity in and from which the universe appears, you are empowered beyond compare. In fact, you are the power behind all that is. You lose fear of the unknown because nothing is unknown. You lose fear of dissolution because, as No-thing, you are nothing to begin with, and as Everything, you are, well, everything!

Love becomes possible. Vanishing here as a "self," you make room for "others," and joy emerges. Humor flourishes, for what could be sillier, more ironic, than this banter between Self and Self? What comedy or tragedy could surpass this wondrous play of Being?

Anger may arise, but never hate. Sadness and grief may appear, but not despair. Seeing everything inside you, where is there cause for greed or envy? Even your troubles are blessings, invitations to return to Who You Really Are where no troubles, no mistakes exist.

And where once again you are reminded that ultimately there are no "improvements," not at the level of your human appearance nor at any other level, for Who You Really Are is whole and wholly perfect, exactly as you are. For how, as

Aware No-thing, could you possibly improve who you are when you are literally nothing, no *thing* that could change? And how, as All Things Appearing In Aware No-thing, could you change when you are all possible changes and all that could be or not be changed? Where even the idea of improving your*self*, the urge that originally brought you to the mystics and seers, is finally seen for what it is: Who You Really Are dancing with Who You Really Are.

It was, after all, never about "you."

CHOICE

Do you have free will? Can you choose what you like and avoid what you don't? Is it built in, as you suppose? A God-given right?

Consider this: When you meditate, can you stop your thoughts for more than a minute or two? Can you control the content of your thoughts? Are you even sure they are *your* thoughts to begin with?

Or this: The scientific description of perception includes the odd fact that you are living in the past. By the time light reflects off an object, even a nearby object, and enters your eyes where it is then processed into electrochemical messages and sent along the optic nerve to the brain, a fraction of a second has elapsed. What choice could you exercise in the present moment if the moment has already passed by the time you are aware of it? Or are you living in a future that is already determined and about which you can only surmise? By the time you are aware of anything, even this thought, is it not already gone?

And this: Science says that the bodily impulse to act – to move your hand, for instance – occurs an instant *before* you think "move hand." If you are not choosing to move your hand, who is? How is it that before you choose to do anything your body is already doing it? Are your thoughts redundant? Are "you" perhaps redundant?

Did you choose your gender? Did you choose your parents, your environment, growing up? Did you choose your life, including all of the losses and disappointments along the way, and would you choose them again if the opportunity arose?

How is it you are certain you have free will, when the

evidence suggests otherwise? It seems true; effect seems to follow cause, but is it real? If the ego is no more than an idea, a bundle of thoughts and feelings centered on the body, then who really is choosing? An idea? A bundle of thoughts that call themselves "you"?

Free will seems valuable because to lose it is to lose the "self." Or so it appears. To remain who you think you are is to the ego a matter of life and death. So if you hear from a spiritual teacher that there is no choice, you might then go around deliberately trying not to choose, or interpret "no choice" to mean "going with the flow," passively accepting "what is" and trying to live "in the moment."

But there is all the difference in the world between passively accepting "what is" as who you *think* you are, and actively intending what happens as Who You Really Are. The former is a recipe for frustration; the latter is freedom itself.

"Then I'll drop the idea of a separate self and become Who I Really Am," you say – as if you, a bundle of thoughts, could choose to do so, as if you could drop decades of conditioning just like that. No one drops anything precisely because there is no separate one who could do so. The human being you identify with is a completely conditioned aspect of the Whole, is an appearance of Who You Really Are, and as such can neither choose nor act on its own. And it is not a question of free will versus determinism, for neither applies to Who You Really Are, which is No-thing/Everything. As No-thing, there is no one who could choose and nothing that could be determined. As Everything, what could exist apart from the All to choose or be chosen, determine or be determined?

If you believe you are a separate self, the discovery that you have no choice can he freeing indeed. It means that you have never made a mistake, that every act and every thought has been conditioned by an infinity of forces beyond your control – that in fact you have no control over anything whatsoever and therefore are not responsible for your past. Everything in your life has been perfectly essential. Gone is the guilt for what you thought you had done, gone the shame for who you thought you were. Gone also the need to blame others, for others are no more responsible for their acts than you are.

But this freedom is temporary, for it is an experience of the separate self, the mind and body with which you identify, and like all experiences in and of the world, it doesn't last. It is momentarily freeing, or it may come and go, but it is not the freedom of Who You Really Are, which is not a feeling, not an experience (although it may appear in the body as such), not an event. Who You Are is prior to isolated events, prior to experiences, prior to such concepts as freedom or bondage, free will or determinism. As a separate human being, you are an integral part of an infinite cosmic display and totally at its mercy. As Who You Really Are, you *are* that display.

The difference then – and as always – is in where you place your identity: "out there" with your mind and body, or right Here where you can plainly see you are No-thing. The difference is between being only human and having no choice, or being the One Chooser of all that appears (which you are anyway!). And this identity shift is said to be the result of grace, for who you think you are cannot make it happen – and yet it happens. And when it does, when Seeing sees Itself, that which is chosen is that which *is*, and that which is is that which is chosen. They are not separate. Intent and the result of intent are one and the same, and what you are is what you have always been – the Sole Intender.

See. Look at looking and see that you cannot find another Presence anywhere, that all is within you, that all will is therefore your will. How could it be otherwise? No matter what the thoughts, when are you not Who You Really Are? When are you not the Chooser, responsible for every last bit of Who You Really Are?

EXPERIENCE

Enlightenment is a state of pure bliss that you will eventually attain through meditation and mindfulness and other forms of mind training. It may not happen in this lifetime or the next, but even if it takes a hundred thousand lifetimes, it will happen. And when it does, you will know only joy, love, beauty, pleasure, freedom and fulfillment. You will finally be awake. In the meantime, you may have "glimpses" of enlightenment, and these experiences will help to spur you along, help you to drop your defilements and train even harder to become a perfect being. And the best part is, all of this will happen to you, to yourself, for how else could enlightenment be experienced if you aren't there to experience it? When you are enlightened you will know it, you will feel it, you will live it!

The above is at best an exercise in wishful thinking and at worst a message of profound ignorance. And yet millions of people believe it to be true. So what's wrong with it?

The Buddha taught "no-self." He claimed that our essence, like the essence of all phenomena, is emptiness. This "void-nature," he said, is what we really are, and realizing what we really are is the end to our suffering.

If there can be a definition of enlightenment, then according to the Buddha it would have to be that there is no one to be enlightened! If what you are is emptiness, who is this "you" to be enlightened? Who is there to experience bliss or, for that matter, to experience anything at all? The sanskrit word *dukkha* is translated as "suffering," but might it not also be taken to mean "experience," as in "suffering experience"? Enlightenment, then, as the "answer" to experience, cannot be an experience. It is no-thing. It is awake and empty Space prior to thoughts and feelings.

Unlike thoughts and feelings, including joy and suffering, Who You Are does not come and go. The question is, are you that mind and body having those experiences, those sensations and thoughts and feelings? Or are you the awake Space in which they happen?

This is not to say that experiences don't appear to happen, that thoughts and feelings and events are not experienced. They do appear to happen, but do not define Who You Are, and are not "yours" as who you think you are. Here at the center of the universe where you are, there is simply nothing. Clean, clear awareness and nothing else. No mind, no thoughts and feelings, no experiences. Looking to see confirms this. Here, you are truly mindless, and all that you once considered "yours" – your thoughts and feelings, your experiences—are seen to be "out there" in the world. The distinction is crucial, for when you see that here you are free of experiences, you see you are free of the grasping and aversion that goes with them, free of saying, "I did or felt this, this happened to me," and thus free of defining yourself as a thing among things, a separate self and no more, an ego in constant need of reinforcement in the form of "personal" experience.

Crucial also because, free of experiences, you are free to *be* experiences. Not to *have* them, but to *be* them. Being room for them, you *are* them. You are simultaneously the One Experiencer and all that is experienced. No longer having a mind as a separate thing, the world is your mind. The world manifests moment by moment as all physical and mental phenomena, and it is Who You Really Are, manifesting. Experiences are then more vivid, more beautiful, more precious, when there is no "you" here to claim them as your own. They are not then "your" experiences, but What You Are, functioning, expressing Itself.

But, you say, it is so much better to actually *experience* What I Am rather than to read about or be told What I Am.

True, and this is the value of Seeing, of the Vision as opposed to the Word. And it is also true that Seeing is not an experience like other experiences, in that it is always the same, is cool, impersonal, altogether out of time, and does not happen to an "individual."

So you are Space for the world, for experiences, and all that comes and goes in this Space is what you are, manifesting. It is once again a matter of where you place your identity – "out there" as only one of your appearances (in the form of the mind and body that others see and say you are); or right here as this empty and aware Space filled with the scene (including whatever objects and thoughts and feelings, whatever appears to be happening that constitutes "experience").

The above, of course, *tells* you what you are, but only you can *see* what you are. Looking to see is the answer. Words fall away in the immediacy of the vision. As to your experiencing enlightenment at some future date, awakening does not, will not, cannot happen *then*. It is immediate and timeless. And awakening does not, will not, and cannot happen to a "you," to who you think you are (no matter what you think). Enlightenment isn't a happening. It is who you really are. So there is nothing special about enlightenment; it is not a wondrous and unique event. It is that which you have always been: empty aware space filled with the world. It is that which you cannot not be! It is the recognition of This-Right-Now by This-Right-Now, and there is absolutely nothing that is not This-Right-Now.

Source, No-Source

Why is What I Am the source of everything that is? Because what else is there? What could there be to be apart from What I Am? Consciousness is the source of everything because there is nothing that is not Consciousness. There are not two here – source, and other than source. Therefore, nothing is really created. So the word "source" is misleading, for there is no thing here creating another thing there. The drama appearing on a movie screen is not created by the screen. It appears there, oned with the screen. In the same way, everything that is, is What I Am, "appearing" here on the "screen" of awareness. Actually, it is not really "appearing." It is as it *is*, exactly as it is presented, and is What I Am.

The same is true of "becoming." How can I become what I already am? How can I become awake when there is only Awakeness, when there is no separate one to awaken? Awakeness just is. Presence is always present, is never absent, and cannot therefore *become* Presence. So the belief that "someday I'll become awake" is erroneous.

But this reads as gibberish to anyone who thinks he or she is separate from Presence, from Oneness, from What I Am. It is as if Oneness pretends it were twoness, so that a world appears, and suffering appears, and love appears, and perhaps the "return" and the "understanding" and the "Beatific Vision" appear – or perhaps not. It could be said – as if there were two – that you are aware Space or Room or Capacity "here" for everything that appears "out there," thereby emphasizing that which you have been conditioned to overlook – your aware emptiness "here."

Instead of fixating on objects out there as we are accustomed to do, the directive is to "Look back at what you are looking out of," turn your attention inwards upon itself, attend to this empty aware Space you are coming from. And upon seeing empty awareness – and it can be seen – it is also seen to be "filled," to be oned with that which appears "out there," so that void and form are now seen to be void/form: not two, not separate. Thus all that is, is "empty" of selfhood, of intrinsic existence, and is not apart from this empty Space, this aware Capacity for all that is.

This is what you really are. You are not simply what you think you are, a separate person with a separate consciousness inhabiting a separate body. This is merely a belief handed down by parents and peers and reinforced by society second by second all of your so-called "life." What you really are is Presence, Emptiness, God, Buddhamind, Atman-Brahman, Consciousness, Self, and all the terms attempting to name the unnameable no-thing/everything that you are. In fact, you are not even alive. All of your aliveness is in that which fills you, which in its totality is the universe itself. You are pure empty awareness, and your body is the scene, or world, that "appears" in that awareness. Who you think you are as a separate person is thus replaced by the scene, ever changing, appearing and dis-appearing in the forever now-awareness that you are. You are simply This, said to be "functioning" as anything and everything that is. You are the source, no-source of nothing but yourself, and you are no-thing/everything.

WHATEVER YOU SAY

Whatever you say I am, I have to agree with. Call me any name in the book, I'm it. Throw the whole book at me, I'm the book. Here in this transparency, who is there to resist? My only "who" is where you are, is you and what you make of me, is my "truth" for as long as it lasts.

The way it works, the more I defend a self-image, the more I am challenged. The more I resist, the more I am attacked. What I make of myself I project onto the world, and back it comes, often threefold. Thus, believing I am a mind encased in a body, I believe there are "others" with minds in bodies, and automatically I am in a position of confrontation, separate and alone. Believing I own the thoughts I experience, I believe that others own thoughts as well – about me. I grow afraid, defensive, angry, learn to manipulate, to role play, to get what I can while pretending to be civil. I am "fallen." I am living in "sin."

But without these beliefs, I am What I Am – transparent awareness, filled with whatever arrives, which happens to be Myself appearing as "other." Then there is no projection, for there is no world other than What I Am.

And it is not a matter of adopting new beliefs. Without the lie, I am What I Am – it is my natural state. However, even *with* the lie, I am What I Am, though I don't see it. So it's not a matter of getting rid of old beliefs either (as if I could). What I Am is prior to belief, and can be seen regardless of the thoughts that come and go, and once it is seen, the beliefs may lose power immediately or may hold sway for years and then abate slowly, may even seem amusing or comical, like stubborn old friends. The point being, they are not the point. They are not Who I Am, they appear *in* Who I Am.

And because they show up here as part of the world, the fact remains that I am the author of those thoughts and beliefs and the world they both create and happen in. There is no separation here. It is all Who I Am. I am responsible for the Whole of it, and I revel in the perfection of it, the precision, the beauty. It is Who I Am, mirroring Who I Am, turning Itself back again and again with a smile. Reaping what I sow, I fall so that I might rise and know that I have never fallen, have not for a second as the Son strayed from the clarity of the Holy Spirit or the arms of the loving Father. Form is void and void is form, and What Is is What I Am.

The truth is: Whatever you say I am, I say about Myself.

KNOW THYSELF

Who are you? How well do you know yourself? Growing up, did you think that everyone but you knew who they were, knew what they wanted? Do you know yourself any better now? So who are you, really?

And if you say you are no more and no less than a human being, consider the fact that the body you say is "you" is made up of billions of individuals called "cells," each alive and cooperating as a whole in such a manner as to boggle the mind of science itself, a veritable world of your so-called "parts" operating below your level of consciousness, with no input from you. Your circulatory system, your digestive system, your immune system – do you know how you do it, can you keep track of these comings and goings?

Or how about your genes, your chromosomes? Who are you at the molecular or atomic level, how do these trillions appear and disappear and hold together under your name, and is it you who are reading this sentence or is it the combined effort of a multitude so vast as to defy the imagination? How did they follow what was said?

For that matter, where do your molecules and atoms end and those of the world begin? How do you draw the line separating what you call "you" from the endless continuum of wavicles you call the "universe"? Do you think of yourself as a question of density, a walking, talking demonstration of mass-energy equivalence? Or as an apparition of probabilities, a living world of sub-atomic particles whose brief and mysterious visits somehow depend on the presence of an observer? And who is this observer?

But perhaps you can best be defined by that which you need in order to be you. Certainly you need all of your inner subordinates and their workings – quarks to organs – but so too the outer: the air, water and sunlight, the earth to nourish you. And what if there were no galaxy, no universe? Why would you call all the matter and energy inside your flesh body "yours," and all the matter and energy outside "not yours," when you need both to survive? Put another way, why limit yourself to the scope of touch and taste, and claim that certain smells and sounds and sights are "outside" you, when in fact your body extends as far and wide as you can smell or hear or see? Senses are global, and so is thought. All that you can possibly think of, all time and space and all that lies within them is your body, is inside you.

Is the universe conscious? Yes, because you are conscious. Does the universe see and hear and taste and feel? Yes, because you see and hear, taste and feel. Does the universe display intention? Of course – because you do, in whatever form it takes. Your true body is the universe, and all that happens is you, happening. Why pretend otherwise, when what you are is so blatantly obvious?

Know thyself!

SEEING

It's everything, and it's awake. It doesn't know how or why it's this way, or why it is at all, or even what "everything" or "awake" is. Perhaps all it can say of itself is that it's not absent, or is the sort of absence – the absence of absence – that can only be presence.

But what is it? Why does it keep asking itself this question, and answering it with laughter? Or joy? As if it could be anything other than what it is!

It looks, and sees only itself, weaving thoughts into patterns appearing as "other." But what does it mean to "look" or to "see"? What is this act of seeing? How could it be other than the all of everything – the infinite universe – seeing itself via itself, so that the "participation," if you will, is infinite? Infinite, and timeless.

Science's story is that light from the sun is reflected from an object and enters the eye of an observer, passing through the lens and forming an upside-down image on the light-sensitive cells of the retina, where it is transformed into electro-chemical impulses which travel along the optic nerve to the visual cortex in the brain; there, the impulses are processed by a host of cells, themselves consisting of molecules, atoms, particles, and so on, until the point of arrival is reached and perception occurs.

This story is one of total participation – from universe to galaxy to sun to planet to object to eye to cells, molecules, atoms, particles, and finally the terminus where "seeing" occurs. And yet the story is merely one of objects interacting with each other, and fails to explain how anything is actually "seen," i.e., experienced. How is it that one set of objects – the cells, molecules, atoms and particles of the

21

brain – is arbitrarily set apart and said to "see" another set of objects (say, flowers in a garden), when all of the objects in question interact as a whole?

The story explains only how objects interact, and not how perception is actually experienced. Assuming the presence of a "subject" here with which signals from an object "out there" are said to interact, the presumption is made that, at a certain critical threshold, "subject" *perceives* "object," as if one object (referred to as "subject") could perceive another, with no proof of how or where awareness is generated or what part it plays in the transaction. Science, in order to make sense of how we experience the world, thus splits the oneness of Subjectivity into the duality of subject and object, reducing subject to the status of object and in the process altogether mystifying the act of perception.

The truth is that Oneness, the All, is the Observer, that perception occurs only to and by the All, "internally," within Itself. Oneness is viewing Oneness, and in order to do so, presents Itself as "other." But there is no other. "Other" is strictly Oneness, so that there are no intermediaries, no separate "beings" with eyes and brains that perceive, no one and no thing to get in the way of the immediacy of seeing. The true observer is the Whole, and the Whole is no-thing/everything, awake to Itself. The circumference is thus the center and the center is the circumference, and only THAT sees, hears, feels, is aware. So that when "I" see anything, I as the Whole see that which is presented, which is Myself – *exactly as it is presented*. That which is presented is in reality not something else, is not a shadow or a representation of Myself – it *is* Myself, the Whole, seeing Itself. Seeing is therefore unmediated, all at-once, now – as is hearing, touching, tasting, thinking, and feeling, all "done" by the All, with no steps, no parts, no passage of time, and therefore not "done" at all. Thus I take what I see: this empty and infinitely spacious Capacity and what it contains, fully aware of Itself, all right here. Once again, it is none other than Who I Am.

DING-DONG

"God is free to rid Himself of God."

D.E. Harding

Occasionally the question arises, "How do I bring this Vision into my life?"

And the answer is: It is already in your life, it is what your "life" is, it is functioning, manifesting right now as what you think is "you, having a life."

John Daido Loori, abbot of Zen Mountain Monastery, once said that what you do and what happens to you are the same. And this is because there is no separation. Your body and mind and the "life" you live are manifestations, apparent "happenings" of Who You Really Are: the Whole.

So from the point of view of the Whole, the notion of bringing Who You Are into Who You Already Are is patently absurd. It is pretending to be apart from Who You Really Are, and then attempting to transfer the vision of Who You Really Are to this pretend part so that the pretend part might live as Who You Really Are! As if, once having had a glimpse of Who You Really Are, you could incorporate it into who you are not! As if you could permanently "do" or "have happen" that which is happening anyway. As if you could bring that which is timeless into time and somehow "live" it.

But, as a friend said recently, "It is the very nature of it to be apparent and hidden at the same time. It is the basic structure of living as human and divine – finding it, and then being swept up by life's distractions and losing it, then finding it again."

And so we go back and forth, realizing and forgetting, Seeing and not Seeing. It is what Douglas Harding called the "ding-dong": the relationship between Who You Really Are and who you think you are. And it is this relationship between No-thing and Everything that gives rise to the universe, that *is* the universe. Harding states:

"The price of a universe is this ding-dong. It's the price of a universe that the individual parts shall, as it were, pretend to be God. They pretend to be real and self-sufficient and self-contained. It's a mistaken view, but without it there's no story, no universe."

Thus we see Who We Are, and we forget. And then we berate ourselves for forgetting, which solidifies all the more the mistaken view that we are separate individuals apart from the Whole, in this case individuals who should be able to live as the Whole. This back and forth relationship is time-based, and is strictly from the point of view of a separate individual, the view that Harding calls "mistaken." Mistaken because the not-Seeing, the forgetting, are thoughts happening *in* Seeing, *in* Who You Are! You cannot *not* be Who You Are, even when you think you are not.

The key, once again, is to look. It is as simple as looking in the right direction. Are you in your body, or is your body in you? Are you trapped in your beliefs, or are you this free Space that contains them? What is it really like here? Is Who You Are conscious, or is that image you have of yourself conscious, the one you see out there in the mirror, the one others see? What we think we are, we think is conscious, but that image has no awareness, no consciousness. It is simply a story attached to a body, a "third-person" narrative. When you see Who You Really Are, it is not that image who Sees, who makes the realization, it is Who You Are who Sees – the only Seer there is! You think it is you who Sees and forgets, but it has always been the One Seer,

God, Self, Emptiness, The Beloved who Sees and forgets to See, who does (or *is*) all that is. Therefore, *trying* to See is counterproductive because Seeing is Being Who You Really Are, and Who You Really Are is effortless. It embraces all that appears, including forgetting. Including, even, trying to See.

When this is understood, the image, the person, the individual with your particular name and form, the body that "follows you around" in all your waking (and dreaming) moments, is seen for what it is – a unique and indispensable element of the Whole, an element without which there would *be* no Whole.

So look after that body and mind you sometimes think you are, the one you call "you" when you forget Who You Really Are. Bring that "you" into Who You Really Are and be the joy, the gratitude, the love that flourishes between you as No-thing and you as All Things, you as Empty Awareness and you as the one among many that fills it. After all, you designed it this way; it is the nature of your business as God and God Incarnate. It is, after all, not a question of bringing It into your life but of a life lived *from* It. Be THAT.

HEAVEN AND HELL

Heaven is not attainable; it is the natural state. Heaven cannot be found elsewhere because it is right here. It cannot be reached in the future because it already is. In Heaven, there is no greed because what you want you already have. There is nothing chosen and nothing done that is not chosen or done by you. In Heaven you are eternal, you cannot die. You can truly live because you were never born.

In hell, you believe you are only one of your appearances – a human being – when actually you are so much more and so much less. Therefore, you continually bargain with reality because you think something is missing. In hell, somewhere else is always better than here, and somewhen else is always better than now. Consequently, disappointment is your companion, control is your game, anger is your prison. In hell, you are trapped by your beliefs, alone, afraid, destined to die. You are who you think you are. You have innocently accepted a story told by others and made it your own.

In Heaven, you are infinite, boundless and free; your "body" and "mind" is everything that appears, moment by moment within the Oneness that you are. In hell, you are limited, small, stuck in a body and mind, merely one among many, apart from and up against a world full of "others," a world in which you must continually strive to gain an advantage, to succeed, to survive. In hell, if you are lucky, you live in a nation where you are guaranteed the pursuit of happiness. In Heaven, there is no pursuit. You are both happiness and sadness and, whichever arises, you abide in joy.

In hell you are awake and don't know it. In Heaven you are Awakeness Itself. Seen from the perspective of hell, the world is abstract, conceptual, vague. From the perspective of Heaven, it is concrete, perceptual, clear. Hell is idolatrous and dreamlike. Heaven is actual and ordinary. The answers you seek in hell are laughably obvious in Heaven – they can be seen in an instant, looking within. In hell, God is an unsolvable mystery worthy only of faith. In Heaven, God is intimately available and openly seen. In hell, confrontation is the norm. In Heaven, it is face there to no-face here, world there *inside* of Awareness here, form and void perfectly One.

In hell you are alone, lonely, poor. In Heaven you are The Alone, filled with the universe, rich beyond measure. In hell you are subject, manipulating objects. In Heaven you are Subjectivity, dancing with Yourself.

In hell, everything is symbolic of something else. In Heaven, everything is as it is. In hell, thoughts and feelings belong to you, and you have pride or guilt. In Heaven, thoughts and feelings belong to the world, while you are clear and aware. In hell, you may be surprised and thankful for something that happens. In Heaven, *you* are astounded and grateful that you have happened.

In hell you are a dream character, a victim of circumstances. In Heaven you are the Dreamer and all that is dreamed. In hell you move through a scene that is still. In Heaven the scene moves through the Stillness you are. In hell, like others, you carry a head. In Heaven you are headless and empty for "others." In hell you are right-side-up with your feet on the ground. In Heaven you are upside-down and the Ground of the world.

Hell is *believing* you are what you look like to others, from where they are. Heaven is *seeing* what you are right where you are: open, transparent, boundless, empty, awake, and filled with the world.

Simply put, in hell you are looking *for* God. In Heaven you are looking *from* Him.

GOD INCARNATE

Heaven, however, cannot be heaven without hell. *Nirvana* cannot be *nirvana* without *samsara*. Why? Because they are not two, not different, are one and the same – yet must be seen as separate, must be distinguished in order to be truly realized. Who I Am is both no-thing and everything.

The emphasis, of course, is on no-thing, perhaps for years, perhaps for a lifetime. How else to break the fixation with the body, the rock-solid belief that we are what others tell us we are – a human being, a separate person and nothing more?

But total identification with our humanity need not be broken (as if it could be). Seeing Who I Am, I see I am also human. After all, being human is one of my appearances, an important part of my world "out there," and it is what others see when they look here. To deny my human appearance, to cut off or suppress thoughts and feelings, is to cut off the world itself, to sink further into ignorance. And the response, when those thoughts and feelings surface again, perhaps this time disguised as physical ailments or "accidents," will likely be harsher, for the balance is always maintained.

Ironically, when we see we are not merely human beings, we become more human. We are free to fully enter the role and be fully responsible for it. How do I know I am not only a human being? I look, and right here where I am I see nothing; I look at looking and see this emptiness big enough for the world to fit into, lit up and awake. Big enough certainly for that human body out there in the mirror to fit into, and all the thoughts and feelings that go with it. I am room for my humanity, and, no longer constrained by the "me" notion, my humanity is free to be what it is, an individuated and interconnected part of the Whole, an appearance in a universe of appearances, and like all appearances, one that the universe cannot do without, for the Whole can only be the totality of all that is, exactly as it is.

But an appearance of what? Of this awake emptiness, this divine void from which I look, hear, touch, am present. And how do I know that my humanity, that the world "out there" is an appearance of Who I Am, which is to say, is Who I Am? Because whatever I go all the way up to, I lose, and all that remains is what I "bring," i.e., this bare awareness, this presence that I am. Everything is Who I Am, lent its appearance by what we call "distance", but it is always seen from here where I am.

Again, I see from here that I am human there. Here – awake Capacity. There – my human manifestation, body and mind. And they are not two. What I identify with, therefore, is this *awake Capacity filled with my humanity*, so that my humanity is seen as a manifestation of This Which I Am, and not the other way around. Here, then, I am impersonal. And until I see that I am impersonal here, I cannot be truly personal there, cannot be fully the individual that I appear to be to others, cannot be distinctly "me." Until I die here, I cannot be truly alive there – and all the while I see and know that there is no "here" and "there," that all is "One" (and not even One).

It has been called the Incarnation, whereby God, the divine Self, incarnates in human form, replete with thoughts, feelings, suffering, joy – all the experiences of being human. God, however, is not ousted. On the contrary, it is *God having the experience of being human*, including forgetting that He is God! Ultimately, all experiences can only be experienced by God, for God is all that is. Said another way: From nothing arises awareness and what it is aware of, two sides of the same coin. Awareness could not be aware without something to be aware of. Light could not be seen without an object upon which to shine. "I" cannot "be" with being "me."

So my humanity is vital, for without it I could not know Who I Really Am. Ego is therefore not an illusion when seen from Who I Am. It is only illusory when I believe it is *all* I am. Seen from Who I Am, ego is not to be rejected; it is overseen, cared for, even treasured for what it is. Seen from Who I Am, my body is not the work of the devil; it is God walking, talking, reaching out with His hands to embrace His world, seeing with His Eye all that is Himself, and finding it to be good. Seen from Who I Am, my human face in the mirror serves the unrivaled function of showing me that here I haven't got a face, that this wonderful tension between truth and illusion is necessary and right, that who I think I am and all the suffering arising from the story of "me" is the divine tap on the shoulder, the call to come home. Imperfection "there" to perfection Here – this is Who I Am alive to Myself, honoring myself. How else could I love? How else could I *be* love?

CALVARY

From this infinitesimal no-point, from this spaceless and timeless no-thing, arises all of space and time, the universe as we know it. And all of space-time, the totality of the history of the universe, from the big bang (or infinite past) leads right to here, to Who I Am exactly Where I Am, which is nowhere in space-time. This is what history is, what History is for, and it ends not in the ambiguous complexity of The Word but with the simplest and most obvious of hand-signals; indeed, it took all of creation to come up with this one index finger pointing back at this no-thing from which all of creation arises.*

Because it is What I Am, the world mirrors What I Am. And it is physical, on display, available. It is not a riddle to be worked out philosophically or mathematically but is immediately available to the senses, is right in front of the face I don't have; in fact, it *is* the face I don't have.

History recapitulates bodily in each of us. The Biblical stories of the Fall, Crucifixion, and Resurrection could not be more current and personal. We need only attend to what is manifestly obvious to know the meaning of revelation and salvation. God couldn't be more demonstrative about what and where He is. Attending to that which is given – not to what I assume or imagine or am told by others, but to what is actually presented – I look up at the sky, then down at the mountains and plains, on down to the sidewalk and my little feet, *down* farther to my foreshortened legs, my giant torso

---

* For the term "hand-signal" and the idea that the end of history is to be found this side of an in-pointing finger, I am indebted to the late George Schloss and his book *The Language Of Silence* (Vols. I and II).

and enormous shoulders. And what do I see below this? I see the cut-off, the end of everything, beyond which there is nothing but clear, luminous Space, aware of Itself. If I hold my arms out to the side I see that they reach to the opposite ends of the universe, and that all that appears between is within this aware Space, including this upside-down and headless body. It is a body unlike any other because it is the body of First-Person-Singular, while all those other bodies are headed, right-side-up third-person bodies. And here, with outstretched arms, attending at the same time to this Space and the scene that appears within it, I see Who I Really Am. I see what Jesus of Nazareth saw, and what anyone anywhere who cares to look can also see – that Who I Really Am, Who You Really Are, is the Son of Man, given a body that is cruciform and dying the only true and total death there is, right here, in and as No-thing, so that the world might live within Him.

Everyone is God incarnate, if he or she will only look, and in so doing die to who they think they are and be born again as Who They Really Are. My upside-down body – the body of Christ, the body He saw then and still sees today – points the way and is the key to the resurrected life. And that way is *down* to the bottom of the world, here where all of the world's suffering weighs on the heart – and then *through* to the Emptiness where I truly am, where I am No-thing, where I am luminous aware Space for everything "up there" to happen in, where God is I and I am God and all is seen to be right. All is forgiven because all that is "up there" appears here in Who I Am, and so is Who I Am. Dying to who I thought I was, I am resurrected as Who I Really Am.

Calvary is present. It is physical, available to anyone. Who is willing to be nailed to the cross and take on the "sins" of the world, to die so that others might live in Him, *as* Him? Who is ready to give up the lie and see the obvious? Who, indeed, is everywhere and does all that is done?

Well, Who is upside-down and reading these words?

BLINK: REVELATION AND SALVATION

What is revealed? Nothing. It has never been hidden, it has always been here. It has been called the open secret because it is not seen, but all along it is what is seeing. And it's not that there is some*one* here and some*thing* there. It is simply *seeing.* The someone and the something are not different from the seeing, *are* the seeing. This is all it is. This is all that is revealed, and it is revealed to no one, to No-thing. Blink, and suddenly it's clear. There is nowhere to go, nothing to do, all is revealed. Seeing simply sees seeing, and we call it revelation.

What is salvation? To be saved is to be taken in by God, forgiven, offered eternal life. But who is saved? An idea, a story? An appearance "out there," one that "others" see from where they are? From the point of view of First-Person-Singular (and really, what other point of view is there?), do I need to "save" one of my appearances, what I already am? Being Him, who but Him is there to save? But of course! This is salvation, the only salvation there is. Blink, and I am saved, for I am already Him. I am revealed to be God by God, and I, God, have saved Myself from "sin" and "death" and given Myself "eternal life" in "heaven," all of which is What I Am, playing all the parts and props of a drama that seems to be other than What I Am. It's a good performance, and then – blink! – it's over.

WITHIN

Jesus said that the Kingdom of Heaven lies within, which may be truer than saying that it lies "without," but in reality there is no "within." Within what? In Oneness, what could be within or without, near or far, here or there? The term "within" is useful only because we identify with the human body and mind and are conditioned to interact with a world we believe is "out there," when in fact What We Are *is* that world, displayed right Here in absolutely nothing, a no-thing that is wide awake to its own presence.

And, of course, this can be seen. Not with the eyes, for the eyes do not see, any more than the hand feels or the tongue tastes or the ears hear. Seeing, like feeling or tasting or hearing, is an act of the Totality for the Totality, requiring nothing short of the Totality to "perform" it. The physical act of seeing is galactic, sidereal, planetary, human, cellular, molecular, atomic, and subatomic, and I say, "I see a flower" (apparent subject seeing apparent object), but in reality there is just "flower," before naming, seeing itself. All of creation is involved, and all of creation calls itself Awareness, calls itself Presence, calls itself God, calls itself "flower." All of creation says I Am – and doesn't know what else to call itself except what appears.

What *is* this? What is going on? There is the urge to ask where it came from or how it got here, but the questions are absurd. Even "always" makes no sense. It is "empty," and yet manifests as the "ten thousand things" – it is the "ten thousand things," but cannot be named as one of them. It is timeless and spaceless but issues forth as all of time and space. It is awake, but appears as a dream. It is aware of itself, but forgets who it is. It is Self, but arises as "other."

It is The Alone, but occurs as the uncountable many. It is divine, but manifests as ordinary. It is Who I Am, but functions as who I am not. It writes these words, and laughs at its inability to describe itself.

In reality there is no such thing as delusion, no such thing as ignorance, although the terms are used to distinguish between Who We Really Are and who we think we are, the former a fact we can see for ourselves, the latter an idea we have learned from others. Believing we are only human, believing we are no more than separate individuals living in a separate world of separate things – this is said to be delusion. But the nature of Oneness is that it manifests as twoness. Without the appearance of many, there cannot be the fact of One. Up and down, hot and cold, self and other, emptiness and fullness – without this apparent duality there would be no story, nothing for Awareness to be aware of. The irony is, the world is not what we think it is. It is not a world of "objects." It is Subject. It is Who I Really Am – Pure Subjectivity – and this is why there is no delusion, no ignorance, because there is no separate one to be separate and therefore deluded, nothing apart from Oneness to be ignorant. Oneness, Pure Subjectivity, Who I Really Am, All That Is is This.

The Kingdom of Heaven is indeed within, but only because there is no "without."

GRATITUDE

God, as clear Awareness, as pure unadulterated Consciousness, has no feelings. And yet from this mysterious and
miraculous Source gushes a seemingly endless supply of
gratitude. But gratitude for what? For Nothing. For Being.
For Presence. For this Emptiness that issues forth as I Am,
and this I Am that issues forth as All That Is. What greater
gift could One give Oneself?

Gratitude for being The Alone. Gratitude because all
that shows up is strictly for Him. The morning sun, the scent
of pine from the nearby hills, the birds, the cars, the buildings, this room filled with color and shape and sound – it is
all for the One who is not and yet who is, is by virtue of all
these things that arise and pass.

Gratitude for this human body and mind, for all that it
does in its own unique way. Gratitude for not being who I
think I am but for being Who I Really Am, from which and
in which and with which this body and mind and all the rest
appear. Gratitude for this "life" I seem to lead, for this sense
of self that is the basis of all I do "wrong" or "right," and
for the Self that resolves wrong and right and all the other
apparent opposites that constitute my world. Gratitude for
this index finger that points the way Home. Gratitude for
all the other reminders that appear in this Space, which
ultimately is all that comes and goes. Gratitude for God's
will which is my will, for intending all I have and having all
I intend.

Gratitude for laughter, for this Cosmic Joke I play on
Myself. Gratitude for this passion about Who I Really Am,
for this all-consuming fire that reveals my core.

Gratitude for this eternal Now. Gratitude for not being

born and never dying. Gratitude because Who I Am is the origin of all that is.

Gratitude for the word "Amen."

PART II

PIE IN THE SKY

I've tried everything, and nothing works. It's been money and women and drugs most of my life. I kept sabotaging myself, you know? And then I got into this spiritual trip and I know the answer is there, but I'm still not happy. It's like I want some kind of lasting peace and fulfillment, but I can't seem to find it.

And?

And I thought you could give me a tip or two on this "waking up" you talk about.

What's that got to do with anything?

Well, I'll be at peace if I wake up. I'll have no more problems.

That's not necessarily true. What You Are is whatever shows up, whether it's peace or problems or anything else.

But Buddhists talk about suffering and the relief from suffering and the way to accomplish that.

Yes, the Four Noble Truths, the "way" of the Buddha. And no doubt that works, especially if you have a long time to pull it off – like a few hundred lifetimes. But there's a catch: At the end of the journey you find out there was no one to travel it. And then you realize there was no journey, that the beginning was the end' and the end the beginning.

And then there's no more suffering, right?

Accidents, calamities, deaths, windfalls, ecstasies, births – all of this happens. What the Buddha was referring to is the unnecessary suffering caused by the erroneous belief that you are a separate and self-existing individual, a notion you learned as a child and now so rigorously defend, which is evident by your quest for peace.

But if I wasn't dissatisfied, I'd never look.

That may be so. It sometimes happens that suffering backs the so-called "self" into the proverbial corner, and an opening occurs.

I hear or read about these enlightened masters, and they all seem so happy and peaceful. I want what they've got, you know?

Well, I can't help you except to suggest the impossible: that you drop the idea of finding enlightenment, so that the idea of a separate "you" who can find it might also drop. Seeking keeps you bound to your idea of separation. The reason it's impossible to drop the idea is that you are not a separate "you" who can do so. It's not in your hands. Seeking is not something "you" decided to do. It's grace. It simply started, and who knows when it will stop? Someone once said that searching for God is like having sex with a six-hundred-pound gorilla – you're not done until the gorilla is done!

And then I'll be awake?

Look, if you want to feel better, see a psychiatrist. If you want a better life, try a motivational expert.

But I've tried those. They didn't help.

Then at least *understand* the idea that there's no separate "you" who can do or get or be anything. The definition of awakening, if there can be such a monster, is that there is no "one" who awakens.

So I'm stuck like Chuck.

Well, I don't know about Chuck....

I'm serious! If there's no way out – and that seems to be what you're saying – then what's the use of living?

The point is, you were never *in*, but you've been conditioned to believe otherwise. As for "the use of living," my guess is that it's to wake up from this dream of separation – but this is God's business, not yours.

So I'll just do nothing, then.

Try doing nothing. You can't even do that. You've been set up, my friend. You think you're a separate self up against a hostile world with which you must continually bargain in order to survive and be happy. You want to be in charge, but reality is not influenced by what you want or don't want. Or, to put it differently, what you want or don't want is already part of the appearance of reality, and you mistakenly believe you've got something to do with it.

Well, if I'm not me, then what am I? I mean, I've got to be something!

No – you're everything.

Everything?

And nothing.

Wait a minute. Which is it, everything or nothing?

Both – but only when you see they are not different. As long as you think you're somebody, I can only describe the world as unreal, an appearance in mind. When you see you're no one and have no mind, the world becomes real – as what you are. There is no doing; there is only Being, and this *is-ing*, if you will, is Nothing/Everything, the great and final Void filled to capacity with all that is, as Itself.

I don't know.... I'm confused. Can't I just be a guy who wants to wake up and find peace?

You can *pretend* to be that. In other words, you can be like a dream character in a dream who decides he's going to wake himself up. You can believe that, but it's silly, no?

Well, frankly, all of this sounds a little silly to me.

And no doubt it is. It's tomfoolery. It's clowning for pie in the sky. But this is what we do until we see no "we," and then it's simply laughter.

THE GREATEST SHOW ON EARTH

*You've said that a good spiritual teacher is one who has nothing
to teach. But suppose a person wakes up to his true nature, and
then teaches others how to do the same based on the method he
used? This is basically what Buddhism is, no? A method passed
down from the Buddha to his successors and eventually to us.*

It's basically what all religions are, but too often the original
message is lost, and people get caught up in the dogma and
ritual of what's left. The value of Buddhism is that eventually one is encouraged to drop Buddhism. There's a Zen
saying that goes, "If you meet the Buddha on the path, kill
him" – meaning that one must turn away from the teaching
and see for him or herself. About the only thing of value
a teacher or a religion can teach is the message that whatever you think you are, you aren't. I can say you are Pure
Empty Awareness and Awake No-thing/Everything all day
long, and you won't have the foggiest notion of what I mean
unless you see for yourself. Say you've never tasted Greek
food, so I go to a Greek restaurant and borrow a menu and
meet you somewhere. I'm going to teach you what Greek
food tastes like by explaining the menu to you? I don't think
so. You may get a general idea based on similar foods you've
eaten, but you'll never know first-hand what it's like.

*But I see all these ads for spiritual seminars and retreats, about
how this person or that person can change your life, how if you
read this book and follow these steps, you'll never be the same.*

Yes, and it's fun for those who enjoy that sort of thing.
People's lives may change, people may never be the same,

45

but so what? People go to seminars and retreats and spend thousands of dollars, and that's fine. But it has nothing to do with What They Really Are. You don't "get" awakened In fact, how can you "wake up" when what you *are* is Awakeness?

So how can millions of people be wrong? Think of the money, the lives, the incredible time and effort that's gone into the thousands of temples and churches. You're saying all of that's a mistake?

I'm saying it's all appearance. The whole universe is appearance, and you are its Center. It's all *your* appearance, and therefore what you are.

And in saying this, you're teaching me what I am!

These are merely words. It's the menu again. Go ahead, eat the menu, then tell me what Greek food tastes like. No – what's happening here is by Oneness, for Oneness, playing the game of twoness.

But how am I going to learn if this is a conversation with Oneness? I want you to teach me.

Okay, let's pretend there are two of us. If I say to you, "I'm going to teach you Awakeness," how arrogant would that be? It would be saying, "I've got it, you don't. Only I can give it to you because you can't be it yourself." It would be saying, "You have to search outside of yourself for it; it's over here, not where you are!" This is too often what is taught, and when you sit at a teacher's feet and follow his path, you're only reinforcing appearance for appearance's sake.

I have to admit that I haven't really gotten anywhere with the different teachings, but you know, it feels good to be on the path.

It's kind of like the "holy" feeling you get after church Sunday morning, only to forget everything that was said by Sunday night.

True. Being a seeker seems a worthwhile and even righteous way to live one's life. But if you're still identified with a separate "you," it's no different than any other way of living life. It's said that the last and most difficult of identities to drop is that of the spiritual seeker. People can get mighty defensive when you question their faith.

Murderous, even.

Yes, there seems to be a fine line between saintliness and sinfulness, which I presume is the Christian story of the fall of Lucifer. If you define "sin" as separation from God, then I suppose that anything you do is sinful, as long as you think there's a separate "you" doing it. That would include saintly acts as well as evil acts. It really is the epitome of arrogance to set oneself up as God, to pretend one is in charge and declare, "I'm doing this, not you!"

I never thought of it that way. Maintaining an ego is denying God.

It's *pretending* to deny God. It's saying, "God's out, I'm in." There's nothing wrong with an ego; it's simply another appearance in the world of appearances. The problem arises when it's seen as self-existing and willful. An ego is merely a bundle of thoughts. It can't *do* anything, it can't act. Only God does anything, and He does it *as* everything. It isn't necessary to get rid of one's ego – as if that could be done – it's simply a matter of seeing one's true identity as the All, and when that is seen, it is instantly seen to be Here. Nothing actually happens, but it's the greatest show on earth!

So there's really nothing to teach.

Never was. Never will be.

NO CREDENTIALS

If you could live your life over and could be anything you wanted to be, what would you be?

Ah, let's see... A water buffalo?

What kind of dumb answer is that?

You've got something against water buffaloes?

No, and I don't appreciate your sarcasm.

You're right, I was being sarcastic, and it was a dumb answer. But it was to a dumb question.

I ask that question all the time, and people don't think it's dumb.

That's because they think they're people.

So what do you think you are?

I don't think I'm anything. Or, I think I'm everything I can think of.

You make absolutely no sense at all.

You're right about that, too. Often to myself.

Well why don't you do something about it?

Make sense? We just left a Buddhist meeting where a little

49

too much sense was made for three hours. Much of which, I'll wager, would have made no sense to the Buddha!

We talked about karma and the Six Realms!

Yes. Karma is a story we tell to explain what isn't happening to begin with. And as for the other, my guess is that the Buddha would have had a good laugh or given each one of us a whack on the noggin – all that business about hell realms and animal realms and God-knows-what-other-realms, and then declaring them "real" to boot!

But the teacher clarified it in the end by saying that the entire Wheel of Samsara *was an appearance.*

Ah! My apologies. I must have missed that part. After a hundred million years burning to a crisp and another half a billion years frozen in ice, one tends to lose the thread.

Why do you even go to these meetings?

I don't know. It moves, and suddenly here it is, a Buddhist meeting! And I enjoy them, especially on those occasions when a connection is made, when a "glimpse" appears. Or every time the teacher says what he has to say and then looks over at one or another of us with a twinkle in his eye as if to add, "How's *that* for a story!"

So you don't think he's serious?

Oh I think he's serious. But I also think he knows exactly what he's doing. By that I mean he knows that the "path" is a game of hide-and-seek, is a method designed to coax one out of believing in them*selves*, and of course, if and when that happens, the student also sees the path for what it is – a ruse, a scam, something to no longer cling to.

You're calling the Buddhist path a scam?

Of course. All paths are scams. All religions are scams. What else could they be?

Sacred. Holy.

Oh horsefeathers! Buddhism – or any other religion – is no more sacred than that pencil on the desk. Or to put it another way: All religions are sacred, but only because anything and everything else is sacred. What is worthy of reverence is the Totality, or Who You Really Are, which is everything that appears, moment by apparent moment.

Okay, but when you start talking about the Totality and all that, we don't get what you're saying, so we need the path. The path helps us to slowly break our attachments to Samsara *and to our egos – even if it takes thousands of lifetimes – and without it we'd be lost.*

Never lost. And this isn't India, or Tibet, or China during the T'ang Dynasty. It isn't our cultural heritage, and much if not all of the ancient path isn't necessary now. We are perfectly capable of seeing and hearing the direct message. Who We Are knows it, hears it, and sees it. One look in the right direction will confirm it.

Part of the reason that religious paths are popular is that they provide something to hold onto, especially when fear arises, when loss of self seems imminent. Plus, they give one something to do, and provide a reason, a purpose, for living. This is all well and good, except it too often accomplishes the opposite of what it intends, which, in the case of Buddhism, is to rid one of attachments. A stronger and more satisfying sense of personal volition, coupled with a "purpose" in life, can only lead away from the goal, more securely pinning one to the Wheel of *Samsara*.

Well, as I see it, we have no choice, because without the Dharma *we'll never get off the wheel, and* Dharma *practice has been honed to perfection for well over a thousand years by several lineages of those who have awakened, from the Buddha on down. It worked for them, and it's the only way it's going to work for anyone.*

My way or the highway? Didn't Torquemada fry 30,000 "heretics" in order to "save their souls" using that same logic? Is that the message of the *Dharma,* or is that the message of radical fundamentalism?

It's what I believe, and it's what I hear in the teaching. I put my trust in the enlightened masters who have handed down the message directly from the Buddha, not in someone who has no credentials and who makes off-the-wall comments and snide remarks. Next, you'll be asking me for money and telling me to wear a pendant around my neck with your picture on it!

No, not likely. Why are you so angry?

Because you're basically telling me that I'm an idiot and that my religion – your religion as well – is full of crap. Last week you told me that the answer to everything is here, but I don't know where "here" is. When I look here I see myself and whatever is around me, and I don't see answers. I try to get into a good conversation about Buddhism with you, and I get crazy shit instead.

And this is the reason a path is needed – is this what you're saying?

Yes. Something I can work with.

Shall we keep it workable, then?

Okay. But give me a minute. I need to cool off.

GIFTS

I'm plagued with questions about things like how and why the universe came to be – the big bang and all that – how and why anything exists, and whether or not there's some outside force directing it all. You said previously that life is a gift, but who is it a gift from? I can see the value of questioning everything, but the more I do, the less I seem to understand. If someone were to ask you for a concise explanation of what all this is, what would you say?

You mean if you were to ask?

Yes. If I were to ask.

Well, in that case, I'd he asking myself, so I'd damn well better answer!

Okay....

The essential understanding is that there is nothing separate, and no separate self. The essential understanding is that everything that appears is a metaphor, a reflection of What You Are, is You appearing to You. The essential understanding is that there is no time or space, no past or future, no anytime or anyplace that is other than You. There is just This, which is You, *is-ing*. There are no probabilities about to arise nor actualities already gone. There's nothing to believe, there's nothing that could be other than What You Are. You are a mirror, accepting anything, holding nothing, reflecting only Yourself. There's no how or why, there's only You. Where did this gift come from, how is it done, why are

You here, awake to yourself? These questions can only be answered with astonishment. There are no answers, and no one to answer them. But what a gift!

Why is it a gift?

It isn't, but for no reason, there's gratitude. Or if you need a reason, it's a gift because, since you are everything that appears, never is there anything to oppose you. It's a gift because, for absolutely no reason at all, you are aware, and aware you're aware. It's a gift because you can never make a mistake, never have to regret, never have to forgive yourself or others. It's a gift because it's free. It doesn't cost a dime.

Consider even what you think you are. The body and mind, taken together as body-mind, is an amazingly wonderful contraption, don't you agree? Composed of billions of individual cells exquisitely working together in concert, the cells composed of molecules, the molecules of atoms, atoms of particles, particles of quarks – and all of it just now uttering these words about itself! But this is only a tiny part of your real body. Your real body is everything you see, hear, taste, touch, think and feel – everything that can be said to be. Mind is space and time, and your real body is the universe. If there's a greater gift, I'd like to know what it is!

But the body, space and time, the universe – all of this is taken for granted by almost everyone.

Yes. There's a line in the *Tao Te Ching* that reads, "When they lose their sense of awe, people turn to religion." The irony is, they are the religion, they are what they are seeking. The Master, the Lord, is what they are. When this is seen, the simplest becomes the grandest, the common the sublime. Until then, everything is perfect anyway.

Well, the universe seems to work pretty well whether or not we take it for granted. Is this what you mean by perfect?

Yes, of course, because in fact there is no "we." "We" only think we're "we," but we're not. Nor is there a universe separate from "us." There is only This – and don't ask me what it is – and it's perfect.

PLEASED TO MEET ME

I have a few questions about some of the things that were said at the Buddhist meeting today. First, the subject of acceptance came up, and I know they were talking about acceptance of the way things are, but I went off in my own direction with it because all my life I have been obsessed with being accepted, with pleasing others, almost as if I'm living for them. It's like I don't have a mind of my own.

Well, then it might only be a short hop to having nothing at all of your own. You don't anyway. And when this is seen, the desire for acceptance may no longer be an issue.

Don't you ever want to please others?

Pleasing others is pleasing myself, so yes, I love pleasing myself. Do I *need* to please? No. Who is it that needs acceptance from whom? There's no outside. Everywhere and everyone is inside Awareness, and Awareness is what I am. Think of it this way: Imagine that the only universe you're aware of is your flesh and blood, your body, and of course, you know it's what you are. Does your thumbnail need acceptance from your eyelid? Do the hair follicles on your right arm need to please your liver?

That's pretty weird.

It's *very* weird. "Self" versus "other" is a strange concept indeed.

But it's normal. How many people don't *believe they are*

separate selves? One out of a million?

Probably more like one out of a hundred million. But this misses the point, the point being that there really is no one separate to believe they are separate! We so easily fall into the trap of judging others in order to remain safely locked into our limited point of view as a "self." The result is that we call a scarce few "enlightened," and the rest of us "normal." And it's all nonsense.

Yes, but the things you're saying are very rarely heard. Who would understand, except maybe one in a hundred million?

It's hard to imagine that anyone *doesn't* understand. It's so plainly here, so simple, so obviously What Is! You say it's a mystery that almost no-one can get, but the mystery is that *everyone* doesn't get it! And again – all this is beside the point. What This is, What I Am, transcends such conceptual musings. In the absence of anyone separate to get it lies the truth of getting it.

From the point of view of a separate individual, though, there's a huge perceptual difference between those who understand and those who don't, and those who don't are the ones who suffer, sometimes a great deal.

Yes. And there are occasions when the dream hits home, when tears there become tears here – and never is there a thought that the situation giving rise to the suffering should be different than it is. THIS appears as suffering, and it *is* suffering, and here, simultaneously, it is complete freedom from suffering.

Is suffering a lesson?

To teach you that you're on the wrong track? To help point

you in the right direction? It could be thought of in that. way, but again, only from the point of view of a separate self. In reality, there are no lessons. As What You Are, you are everything, so where is the lesson and what purpose could it serve, and for whom?

So could we say that suffering is a lesson when it's needed to be a lesson, and when enlightenment happens and there's no longer a character in the dream, it's no longer a lesson and no longer suffering?

We could say that.

But suppose we don't see suffering as a lesson? Suppose we see it the way most people do, as an affront?

Then suffering increases. Hurt turns into anger, others are blamed, lawsuits are filed, wars start–on and on. So what else is new?

It's the story of humanity, isn't it? The Wheel of Samsara.

Yes, and it's exactly what you said it is–a story. It's a narrative we tell, and we call it "real," when in fact, as such, it's a play, a film, a dream. We think we're in charge, but as separate selves we're no more than dream characters, being dreamed.

By whom?

By no one. By Awareness, by This, by What Is, by No-thing appearing as Everything, by God. And not one of those names describes anything at all. Call it the Holy Plunger, if you like. Call it the Perfectly Pure Luminous Lunchbox!

Now you're mocking me.

You mean I'm not pleased with you? Don't flatter yourself. This has nothing to do with your notion of a "you." The conversation has been going in circles from the start, and all the while a finger has been pointing at that no-place where there is no you, at the motionless hub where Presence alone can be said to be.

I'm sorry, but....You mean that figuratively, right? As in, the pointing finger of explanation?

Let's make it literal. Here's my index finger, now it's pointing at what? And right now it's pointing at what?

My face?

Is that what you see—your face?

No, actually.

Look in the direction the finger is pointing. Look back at what you're looking out of, and tell me what you see.

I don't see anything.

But that's where you are! Surely you must see something.

I see nothing.

Is the nothing aware?

Yes, I guess it is, but....

But what?

Could we talk about this later? I've got something else I have to do right now.

Certainly. Apparently I do too.

LOSS

Suppose someone stole all your stuff. I've been thinking about what I'd do, because to me there's nothing worse than a jailhouse thief. If that happened to you, how would you handle it?

I'd ask the staff to take the missing items off my property list.

That's all? You wouldn't hunt down the guy who did it?

No.

Suppose you knew who it was?

I might ask for it back, I might not. Either way, there would be nothing wrong.

Nothing wrong? Your stuff would be gone, and he'd be responsible for it!

No one is responsible for anything.

I'd have to bust his head, if he stole my stuff. I can't believe you'd let him off the hook.

Stuff is just stuff. There's no loss. Who am I to say? Who is supposed to have what? Who is there to have anything anyway?

You'd probably thank him!

I might. After all, he'd be relieving me of what was no longer supposed to be here. It's not possible to steal something from another. Stuff just apparently moves. I don't own anything, nor do you. You just think you do. If there's anything I own, it's the entire universe, because I find it inside this Pure Awareness that I am. Why get all worked up over what can't possibly be lost?

Okay, suppose a friend dies. You wouldn't consider it a loss? If my girlfriend died while I was in here, I'd go crazy.

No one ever loses anyone. No one ever had anyone to begin with. Your girlfriend is you, you just don't realize it. My son died a few years ago, and I know without a doubt that he never went anywhere, and that I never lost him. He's here, he's What I Am, and love flourishes in him. Even on the scale of relative appearance, loss is gain. Losing my possessions, I gain the lightness of having less, or the possibility of something new or different. I always have exactly what I'm supposed to have. I know this because I see and hear and feel what I'm filled with. If it isn't here, it isn't supposed to be.

I can't understand how you don't consider your son's death a loss. Something like that would kill me.

Why would I consider his total freedom a loss? No longer in the prison of his mind or body, he is unlimited awareness. Why would I grieve over that, and what exactly would be the motives behind my grief? Would I not be grieving *my* loss? Would I not be grieving for myself, clinging to thoughts not of him but of how *I* will be without him, or how I failed him, how I did this or didn't do that? Should I blame him for my suffering? If your girlfriend died, would you grieve *her* loss, or would it be all about you and *your* loss? My guess is that it would be the latter.

62

You hardly know me, so you don't know what it would be!

By what you say, I know that you believe you're someone, and when anyone thinks they're someone, they do their best to maintain and protect that image. I too spent most of my life rigorously defending the self I assumed I was. It was very painful. It was all about me, even when it appeared to be about others.

Wait a minute – you don't think you're someone?

No, I don't think I'm someone.

Well, what the hell are you, then?

The same as you – Aware No-thing filled with everything.

Hey, bud – I don't mean to be disrespectful, but you're a little out of your tree. I thought you were a pretty religious guy because you're always so calm, but now I don't know what to think. You need to get ahold of yourself, you know?

I'll take that into consideration, although getting ahold of myself might be a little difficult at this point.

Well you'd better do something, because that bullshit about being nobody is way too weird.

I'll look into it. Thanks for your suggestion.

A MATTER OF LIFE AND DEATH

How would you prefer to die?

Let's see…. Spontaneous human combustion sounds good.

Oh, come on! Can't you ever give a straight answer?

I can, but not to a question like that.

What's wrong with it? Some people would prefer to die in their sleep, some on a golf course, others at home surrounded by family and friends.

What I am isn't alive, so how could I die?

Oh no, here we go again. So all of us will die sooner or later, but you won't!

Correct. All of you, as appearances of What I Am, will age and eventually perish, but I am prior to birth and death. Birth and death are simply chapters in the story of life. Anyone can say this.

I can say it? I'll live forever?

No, you will not live forever. As who you think you are, you will sooner or later die like everyone else. As what you really are, however, you were never born, so how can you live forever if you're not alive?

Okay, I can say I won't die, but I can also say that you will.

Exactly. As your appearance, this human you refer to will age and perish, and so will everything else – people, plants, planets, stars, galaxies – all will eventually pass. But you will not.

Well, what am I, then?

Nothing. That is, nothing that can be objectified. Nothing that can be seen, heard, or touched as you would see, hear, or touch anything you can think of. And at the same time, you are everything that appears – all of time and space is what you are. You have been called Tao, God, Buddhamind, Beloved, Absolute, Sat-Chit-Ananda, Basic Empty Awareness – yet none of these are what you are. You are, as a seer friend in San Francisco once said, the Unfigureoutable.

"Seer" as in someone who predicts the future?

No. "Seer" as in sees-what-is.

But if you can't name it, how can you see it?

Quite easily, actually, as long as you aren't looking "out there," and as long as you aren't looking for anything you can imagine is anything. By that I mean that you must put aside everything you have learned, and see as a little child would, totally open to what is presented, as it is presented, with no preconceptions.

People aren't used to seeing what they are. Most don't know what looking "within" means. So there are devices which lead the presumed looker back to what is looking, and at first it can be a startling experience simply because we aren't accustomed to noticing our Clarity. But really it is quite ordinary, and in fact, not an experience at all, for *seeing* what you are is *being* what you are, which is outside, or rather, prior to the notion of time.

One such device is this piece of cardboard into which I've cut a head-size hole. Try this: Hold it out in front of you at arm's length and look at the hole. How would you describe it?

I don't know – it's oval-shaped, and the hole itself is empty; there's nothing there.

Now bring it toward you ever-so-slowly, noticing carefully what happens.

The hole is growing larger. It's still oval-shaped, but the closer I bring it, the larger it gets.

Keep going. Slowly.

Okay… it's getting even larger… and now the edges of the hole are beginning to blur… and now the hole is huge and I can barely see any of the cardboard….

Now bring it all the way in and put it on.

…Whoa – that's weird! It's like I put on the hole. It's like I am the hole!

How would you describe that?

Enormous. Edgeless. It's not really anything, but it's lit up.

And where is it?

Where? I don't know what you mean. It's here. Where else could it be?

And would you say it's awake?

Yes! Oh, that's really *weird!*

You said it's like you *are* the hole.

Yes, yes, there's no doubt about it.

Okay. Hold it out at arm's length again, and this time tell me what you see *in* the hole.

Okay...I don't see anything. It's empty. Unless you mean part of the room beyond...oh, I see what you're getting at – the hole is filled with a section of the wall, the desk, the stool, items on the desk, and so on.

Yes. Now very slowly bring it toward you, and watch what happens.

The hole is growing larger, and there is more and more of the room in it.

Keep going – slowly – and once again bring it all the way in and put it on.

I see more and more of the room... and now the edges are blurring... and now it's all the way here and there's just the room.

So you've put on the empty hole, the "lit up nothing," as you described it, *and* you've put on the scene inside it. Which are you, then – the awake nothing, or the scene?

Both! They're the same!

That's what I see when I look within. I am nothing and everything, void and form. Better said as nothing-everything, void-form. I am empty capacity for the passing show that fills it. I am edgeless and boundless Clarity, filled to the brim with all that presents itself. And I am aware. Aware even of being aware. And where am I? Here. This is the only place – and it's not a place – I ever am.

Now put the card down and spread your arms out wide. Move them forward until you can barely see your finger-tips in your peripheral vision. You are now holding this enormous emptiness that you are, into which anything and everything imaginable fits with ease, into which the entire universe may come and go. This is what you are. You are capacity not only for the flesh body you see when you look down, but for this vast, vibrant world that appears within you. This is your real body. This is what you manifest as.

Now tell me, as Empty Capacity, as No-thing Whatsoever, what could there be to suffer birth or death? And as Everything – not as a part in a universe of separate parts, but as All That Is, all at once – how could you suffer birth or death? The notion is absurd.

Yes, I see what you mean. I guess it's a matter of changing shirts, so to speak. Of dropping the idea that I'm an individual and adopting this new belief.

No, no. That would be to replace one story with another. It's a matter of getting your identity straight, yes, but this isn't about *believing*, it's about *seeing*, actually looking and *seeing*. This seeing what you are is being what you are, and is prior to belief. Forget the words, the logic of it – forget everything I said, and just *look*.

Okay.

Okay.

THE ALMIGHTY MACKEREL

What is this?

You've got me!

Sometimes I look here, and I just shiver. Does that ever happen to you?

Not any more. Usually it's laughter, or a sort of gushing.

Gushing?

Yes. It has to do with recognition. It's like a pool of gratitude that comes welling up.

But it's self-recognition.

Oh yes. There's no separation.

So what's there to be grateful for? Gratitude requires someone to be grateful and something to be grateful for, no?

No. This is Self-love. It's being in love with everything, and you are everything. It's No-thing grateful for everything it is in manifestation, everything it appears as, which is everything. Don't ask me how this happens.

Okay, how does this happen?

Ha!

I'm serious – I want to know what this No-thing/Everything is. I know there are dozens of names for it, and I guess the word that holds the most meaning for me is "God," but that still doesn't tell me what it is, and anyway, how could I be God?

How could you *not* be? And how wild is it that God wants to know what He is! God has no idea how He Is-es! Every fraction of an instant God pops Himself up out of nowhere like a jack-in-the-box, pulls Himself out of zilch by His own bootstraps and goes, "What is this?" How amazing is that!

So He amazes Himself, too.

Yes!

This is insane.

No, solely identifying with a separate self is what is insane. I don't know what I am, but I show up as anything and everything, all right here, always awake, always Myself. How do I *do* that? There could be just nothing at all, but instead, there's Is-ness! That there's anything, even if it's No-thing – *especially* if it's No-thing – is astonishing.

God is astonished by His own presence?

You bet. I am Nobody, and look what I do! How could I not be stupefied by What I Am? Not to mention grateful.

Would you say you are self-centered?

Oh totally! With a capital "S." This is a love affair of immense proportions, bursting from No-thing, vanishing into No-thing, all by and for Itself. How could God not love Himself when He *is* love – and here's the catch – do so by recognizing and loving Himself as *other*? How could He not be astonished, or grateful?

So if someone says they are enlightened, and there's no astonishment or gratitude, should I doubt their claim?

Anyone who says they are enlightened is probably full of beans to begin with, since enlightenment is defined as the absence of anyone to be enlightened! But your question sinks back into the game of separation – this person or that person experiencing this or that. This is why I like the term "First-Person-Singular." What you are is The Alone. There's no one else here, my friend. In fact, there's no one at all. Come back. Look. Be what you are. See for yourself if Astonishment and Gratitude are your other names.

If there's no one else here, then who am I talking to?

Yourself.

Man.... This is.... Is this some kind of joke?

Now you've got it!

I'm the joke, aren't I, and I've been playing it on myself!

Because there's no one else to play it on.

Holy mackerel!

Ah, yes. The Almighty Mackerel. Yet another of your sacred names!

UPSIDE DOWN AND BACKWARDS

I don't get why you say that everything is backwards.

Nothing is what we think it is, nothing is as it seems. For instance, you think you're in the world, but the world is in you.

How?

Everything that ever was, is, or will be, happens within Awareness. Everything you've ever thought or will think, everything you've ever seen or will see, heard or will hear, touched or tasted or will touch or taste, everything you've ever learned, every memory, every feeling – it all happens within Awareness, and Awareness is what you are. You can actually *see* this. For example, allow your gaze to relax, and instead of focusing on objects out there in the room, look back at looking. By that I mean, turn your attention around 180 degrees and attend to what is seeing, attend to attending. Take in all of it, including the periphery. Notice that what you are attending to is edgeless, as though you were looking through a glassless window with no frame. See that it's awake, lit up as if from within, and completely empty. Now stretch your arms out to the side and bring them forward until you can just barely see your fingertips, so that you are "holding" this boundless emptiness – and notice that the room, the entire scene, fits within it. So you see, you're not in the room, the room is in you.

I see what you mean.

You say that like you *don't* see what I mean.

No, I see it. Maybe I just don't believe it.

Obviously you don't, because if what you see doesn't raise an eyebrow, never mind knock your socks off, then you don't believe it. The meaning, the understanding of it, is revolutionary, and with a capital "R."

What else is backwards?

Should I go on?

Please.

What is taken for sanity is insanity, what is taken for holy is profane, what is taken for truth is a lie. Searching for God or Self or Enlightenment is searching in the wrong direction; the act of searching necessarily leads away from the goal, which has never been anywhere but Here. You think there are many, but there is only One. You think there is a "there" or a "then," but no such place or time exists. You even think you are right-side-up, when you can plainly see you are upside down....

Wait – run that last one by me again. You think I'm upside down?

No. To me, you appear right-side-up, as I do to you. But you've obviously not investigated what you are or how your body appears to you.

What are you talking about? Am I supposed to stand on my head? What does investigating myself have to do with being upside down?

It has to do with waking up from the dream. It has to do with believing what you see, not what you've been conditioned to see. Here...turn your chair and sit facing me. Now stretch your legs out in front of you, toward mine. Does my body appear right-side-up to you, head above and feet below?

Of course!

And how does that compare with yours? Let your gaze drop slowly from my head to my feet, then to your feet, then continue to *drop* to your knees, your waist, your chest....

Oh geez, I am upside down! I never noticed that before. Or is that some kind of illusion because we're sitting facing each other?

It's no illusion. Look anytime you want, in any position – standing, sitting, or lying down. Using the top of your frame of vision as "up," and the bottom as "down," what you see is feet above and chest below.

It's distorted, too.

You noticed! Feet are small, legs are truncated, chest is enormous. Distance determines size – the closer, the larger – and the size of an object perceived at any given moment is the given size of the object.

But I can measure my foot with a ruler, or that chair over there, and it will always turn out the same.

Of course. And that's because the size of the ruler changes accordingly. Hold the ruler up close to you, and the chair is only three inches wide! We learn that objects are a fixed size and shape, but they're not. They're as elastic as time and space. All of appearance is relative to position, and we

74

assume it's static. Ask a small child how big a high-flying jet is, or a car or a house a mile away.

This is nutty. You're saying that buildings and airplanes and chairs actually change shape and size?

All the time. The illusion of fixed size is just that – an illusion. Turn on your television and notice that what appears as a three-dimensional show is actually presented two-dimensionally on the screen. Depth is learned. When you're lost in the show, you never consider the screen. The same is true of "reality." That which you take to be real is in fact an elaborate illusion. The point here is to demonstrate that nearly everyone unquestioningly believes what they've been told, and no one relies on what they see for themselves, right where they are.

Take, for instance, your ideas about who and what you are. No doubt you believe you're a self-existing individual housed in a body-mind; you take it for granted that you more or less look like others, so you believe you're a human being. But is that true? Close your eyes, and tell me truthfully, *on present evidence only* – without relying on what you've learned or what you assume or imagine – how tall are you? How wide? How many toes or fingers do you have, if any? Where does your butt end and the chair begin, if in fact there's an end or a beginning to anything? What does your body look like?

On present evidence, I'm not sure...

When I do the same, all I can report is these sounds and pressures and thoughts floating through like clouds. I could be a mile wide or as narrow as a pin. I could have fifty toes, six heads, and tentacles like a squid. All I can *truthfully* say is that I am this awake presence and the sensations that come and go within it.

So I think I'm human, but I could be anything.

Yes. The root of the problem is that you think you're a separate self and only a human being, when the evidence, presented to you exactly where you are, proves otherwise.

Well, who is it that does *anything? Who is it who came here to talk to you?*

No one does it. Everything just happens. And if you think you came here – or come or go anywhere – you've got another thing coming. You don't move through the world, my friend, it moves through you!

But if I walk across the room, I'm the one who's moving!

No. It's the room that moves, not you. How could you? – You're everywhere! Which is to say that you never move. Never have, never will. What you are is Stillness Itself. This is easily seen in a car, watching the telephone poles and scenery stream by. But with a little getting used to, it can be seen anywhere, in any situation. When walking, for instance, looking down – feet and legs move, arms swing, sidewalk and lawn float by "top" to "bottom," while you – Empty Awake Awareness – remain perfectly still. When this becomes the "normal" way of seeing for you, all that was "upside down and backwards" will be "right-side-up and forwards." And no longer will there be a "you."

COMPASSION

As a Buddhist, one of the most important qualities we learn to develop is compassion and caring for others, but you don't talk much about that.

Am I supposed to?

Well, some of the things you say seem a little cold to me, cut and dried, although you don't act that way at all—so I'm wondering what you think about compassion, how you practice it.

I don't practice compassion. What I am – What You Are – *is* compassion, so what's to practice? I'll tell you what compassion is not: it is not pity, not caring. Pity and caring are business-as-usual, no different than any other exercise in illusory selfhood.

No different than yelling and screaming at someone? No different than socking someone in the eye?

No different. It's all a drama of self and other. Actually, pity and caring can be more insidious because others follow the lead, convinced they are doing good, spreading love, when in fact they are reinforcing the very idea that is the cause of all the suffering in the world – the idea that one is a human being, no less and no more.

Is this the reason Buddhists don't proselytize, don't send out missionaries to convert people in underdeveloped countries?

Could be.

So you really don't care about others?

Why teach worry, anxiety, concern – as if there were something wrong? Why teach separation, when What I Am is All That Is, and All That Is is Love?

Then how do you care? How do you demonstrate compassion?

I already told you. I don't demonstrate compassion, I *am* compassion. Compassion is the heart of All That Is, and it's not a thought or a feeling or a willful act. It's Pure Empty Awareness. It's your nature. Compassion is another name for God, The Absolute, Love. I don't often use the word, however, because it carries too much baggage. Thanks partly, in my opinion, to well-meaning Buddhists exercising wrong view.

I don't see compassion as static, though. It implies some kind of functioning.

Most definitely. It's Emptiness moving. It's No-thing, pouring Itself into Itself, being Everything, being Being.

Yes but this description is vague and impersonal to me, and I want it to be personal, you know?

That's just it, What You Are is both impersonal and more personal than you could ever imagine. To see the personal, you must be the impersonal – which you are anyway, despite what you think.

For instance, right now I look Here and see that I am Empty Awareness filled with the scene, and the scene happens to be you. I disappear in your favor, I die so that you may live. You are all I've got; you are the only "life" I have. If that isn't personal, I don't know what is. I am impersonal Capacity, holding you and All That Is in unequaled personal intimacy.

At the same time, I know without a doubt that your core, your nature, is this same Aware Empty Capacity that I am. Not a *piece* of the same, but the same in its *totality* undivided, absolute. You, right now and always, are What I Am.

So you're saying....

I'm saying, forget the notion that you're only a separate self, and *look!* Look back at what you are. Every answer to every question is potentially in that look. Why listen to me, when you can see for yourself what compassion is?

I listen to you because you are myself!

Ah! Well, in that case – what else is on our mind?

I guess that will do for now, but thank you!

TRUTH IS SIMPLY TRUTH

You contradict yourself. On the one hand you tell people how to see what they really are, and on the other you say there's nobody there who can do it. Why should I believe anything you say?

Please don't believe me. If anything is going to happen, it's going to happen where you are by what you are, not because of anything I say. I can't tell you what you are, but I can tell you what you're not. Only you can see what you are, and it is so simple, so elemental, so close and so ordinary that you miss it.

If it's so ordinary, then why do people all over the world revere it?

Because they misunderstand it. Because, from the point of view of the identified individual, it appears to be special indeed. Because they follow the teachings of those who themselves misunderstand. Because they find a measure of solace in the dogma and rituals of religion, or in what holy men tell them, even though it may lead them astray and reinforce the lie.

The lie being that they are a separate self, an identified individual?

Yes.

But that isn't so bad, is it – being a separate self?

No, not at all. It's all good, as they say. However, it is one thing to know oneself as an appearance in a world of appearances, and another to believe that one is self-existing – to be caught in *samsara*, as Buddhists call it. The latter is the cause of all suffering, all bondage.

Then how can you say it's good?

Because it's the way things are, it's how it is. Without the lie, without good and bad and hot and cold and up and down, there would be no world, and the world is What You Are, manifesting. It's all quite perfect, and perfectly necessary. Even you, as who you think you are – that unique individual body and mind – are one-hundred-percent necessary to the whole, or there would be no whole. That includes anything you say or do, or imagine you do.

Are you including criminals, tyrants, terrorists – the Hitlers and Pol Pots of this world – on your list of "perfectly necessary"? Because if you are, you could be hung in certain parts of the country, or at least run out of town!

I'm including everyone and everything, and you're probably right. My Buddhist friends may see me as lacking compassion, or worse. Others might declare me a sociopath, and one among the criminals on my list.

Does that bother you?

It could, but so what? Sometimes *samsara* hurts, in whatever form it appears. But it is these hurtful moments that bring one back to This, and then it's all wonderfully, beautifully, perfectly good. This too is the way of it.

So you contract into the lie?

Yes. Isn't that wonderful? I get to be a wave thinking I'm a wave with all the other waves, while below me is the infinite sea that projects me, supports me, is my very essence.

But I thought it was a matter of being permanently awake, and living your life that way.

Nonsense. "Permanently" requires time, a past and a future, and What I Am is timeless. There is no "one" to be awake and to have a "life;" Awakeness is what I am. It's been said that the only difference between a person who is awake and a person who is not is that the one knows it and the other doesn't. But even this is untrue because it assumes there are two, and there aren't.

What would you define as truth?

That which cannot be described, and that which has no opposite.

Everything has an opposite.

Except Truth. As No-thing, it has no opposite; as Everything, it has no opposite. It is prior to "true" and "false."

But this is just your way of looking at things, your philosophy.

This is not philosophy. It is not my opinion versus another's opinion. Truth is simply Truth. Opinions and philosophies are what arise *in* Truth, *from* Truth. Truth has no opposite.

And now I expect you'll say that all you just said about Truth is not true.

Amen. How did you know?

82

THE KINGDOM OF HEAVEN

Do you believe in God?

Yes, but not God-as-Santa-Claus.

I'm wondering what it will be like when I go to heaven and see God.

Why not be in heaven and see Him now?

You're joking.

Not this time.

But how is it possible to see God now?

The first thing you need to do is to drop whatever preconceived ideas you hold about what and where God is, and take
for evidence simply what you see in the present moment – in
other words, see as a little child would. Rather than rely on
concepts you've learned from others, accept what is directly
presented. Be your own judge.

Now point at the book on the shelf in front of you. Notice
its shape, color, texture, its solidity as an object. Actually do
this. Go on....

Good. Now point at your foot. Notice that it too is solid,
is a certain shape and color and texture, and being an object,
is therefore similar to other objects in the room....

Now point at your leg, and notice the same....

Now your abdomen... your chest and see that these also
are objects, much as any other object appearing in the scene....

Now point at what you are looking out of. Point back at where you thought you had a face, and tell me what you see....

I don't understand. How can I look at what I'm looking out of?

Point with your finger, and reverse your attention and look at what it's pointing to. We're so used to looking "out there" at people and places and things that we rarely, if ever, look within. Go ahead. Point, and have a look....

Oh Lord – what is that!

Don't ask Him. He doesn't know either.

Why haven't I noticed this before?

Don't ask me. Ask Him.

But I'm....

Him? Yes.

It's like I'm "me," and then when I look within, I'm Him!

You are, as they say, in union with God. Eventually you can drop the "you" and "in union with," but in the meantime it may prevent you from being hustled off to an asylum, and protect the rest of us from an insufferable case of solipsism.

[*One week later*]

This thing you showed me – pointing at where I thought I had a face and looking within – how do I get rid of it?

You want to get rid of God?

84

I keep seeing this all day long, and it's freaking me out. I mean, I've got no privacy!

Welcome to heaven.

CLEAR AS MUD

Were you ever an activist?

A protester? No. I was too busy with my own interests, protesting everything that didn't go my way.

How about now? Would you demonstrate against the war? Racial injustice? Pollution?

I might. I might not.

You don't know?

I don't know what this thing will do two seconds from now, so how would I know whether I'd join a protest, even if I could?

I guess what I'm asking is: What is your position on these issues? It seems to me that anyone who is spiritually-minded would be inclined to demonstrate against injustice, in whatever form.

Fortunately, I'm not spiritually-minded. Not an activist, nor any other kind of "ist." The truth is, there's nothing wrong here, so what's to protest? Why argue with perfection? Why demonstrate against What I Am? If a protest rally appeared, this "me" might well be included, but I would know it for what it was. This may sound harsh, but the truth is that war, racial injustice, and pollution are no more or less important than a leaf falling from a tree. All the sins and tragedies and disasters of this world are in reality the perfection of God, manifesting. Without evil, there would be no good, and no world. All of manifestation is the Son, pointing the way to the Father. It's the holy mirror. It's No-thing dancing with. Itself and calling itself "Everything." What's to protest?

Then let me ask you this: Have you ever given to charity?

Yes.

Would you still give, if the opportunity presented itself?

I might, but it wouldn't be for the reasons I did before.

You mean, to satisfy the ego?

Yes, exactly. To pump myself up. To relieve guilt. To impress others. This is the opposite of giving. It's taking, and a particularly insidious form of it because it poses as genuine care and generosity.

So what reason would there be to give now?

If someone were to ask. If someone thought there was a need. Or for no reason at all. The point is, it's all What I Am, and all giving is giving to Myself. Moreover, all giving is giving Myself to Myself! It appears to happen. Stuff moves. It's kindness, functioning. With no "giver," there's no one saying, "There's something wrong with you; you're a victim; I'll fix you."

Which is a subtle form of violence.

Yes, it is.

So it's a matter of remaining impersonal?

Without the impersonal, it's impossible to be truly personal. Likewise, without the personal, the impersonal is a sham. The reason for this is that they are not separate, not two. There is both, and they are one. Charity is a story, one among an endless parade of stories we tell in order to remain an individual self. But no matter what we think we do, we don't. No matter who we think we are, we aren't. And the story marches on.

You've said that nothing really happens. But we can plainly see that things are happening all the time.

That appears to be true, but if you pay close attention you'll see that each moment, instant by instant, is in fact gone by the time you notice it. When you believe you're a separate self, you believe there's "time" and "space" in which events take place, but space and time are a manifestation of This, which is prior to the concept of a "separate-self-in-space-and-time." All that is, is This. So you see, nothing really happens.

You make it sound like if I see this, I'll disappear!

Well, in a sense, you will. The "individual" you think you are will be seen to be "out there," an appearance of Who You Really Are. At the same time, nothing will change. There you'll be, still wearing your pants – but no longer will you identify with that individual self.

Let's say I see what I really am and don't like what I see. I don't suppose it can be unseen.

No.

Even though 99.9 percent of the world's population doesn't see, once I wake up, I can't go back and join the crowd?

You can, but there will always be the cosmic chuckle in your heart.

And what about those six billion others? How can they all be wrong? Is everybody dreaming the same dream?

That's one way of looking at it, but the truth is that there are not six billion others. There is only Undivided Awareness, and it's nowhere but Here. All of those six billion others appear inside this Awareness, and it is this Awareness that you are. In other words, What This Is, What You Are, appears as "others." Clear?

Clear as mud.

Good. What else?

The reason I sometimes think you're right about me not really being "me" is that I have so many "me's" I don't know which one I am. There are different personalities for different occasions, depending on how I feel, who I'm talking to, etcetera. I think we all have these multiple "me's" – I know I do – but somewhere inside, there has to be a core, a center, that says "I." But I can't put my finger on it, you know?

How could a finger put a finger on itself? "I" is not an object. It is what is looking for itself, and it will never find itself as an object because it is what is looking. The only thing it can find is what it calls actually is itself appearing as other. That's why seeking is a joke. That which is sought turns out to be this which is seeking, and everywhere it looks, it finds only itself.

Clear as mud?

Clear as mud.

Now what?

One more question. I want to believe in reincarnation, but I'm just not sure. What's your take on it?

You're familiar with the expression "You can't take it with you?" Well, the reason for that is that you never had it to begin with.

A self?

Yes. Nobody ever was anybody, so who is it who could reincarnate? There's no one home, no-thing to be here, or to go anywhere or to show up somewhere else. Everyone wants to continue as an individual after death, but they never really were individuals to begin with. Realizing "no-self" before death is termed "waking up," which is an odd term considering that there's really no one to have been asleep, but it sounds good, so we use it.

That said, anything can happen or re-happen in the world of appearance, including people and places and things remembered. Memories, like all thoughts, visual or otherwise, are attached to objects in the appearing world, and as such are appearances themselves. They are not *your* thoughts, they are simply manifesting in Empty Awareness, passing through, perhaps to show up again in apparent time. This is all the play of What Is, and the "existence" you claim as a separate self is but another thought in a vast space-time play of thoughts we call the universe.

But memories are stored in brains.

And what are brains? Are they not objects appearing in Awareness, like everything else?

Most people believe that brains create awareness.

Yes, in an effort to keep our precious selves, we invent the story of objects creating subjects. Science has never been able to prove what awareness is or how it is generated, and we wonder why. Awareness isn't anything to be found inside anything else. It isn't any*thing* at all, and the entire infinite regression of "chicken and egg" is itself an appearance in awareness. Go back, back, back, and eventually you realize that the buck never stops, and that What You Are is in another direction, another *dimension*. What You Are *does not exist* in any objective sense of the word "exist." All you can ever be said to be is anything and everything that appears, which is a function of Empty Awareness, is Empty Awareness *manifesting*. Clear as mud?

Yes. It's all clear as mud.

I hope so. Someone by the name of Ram Tirtha once said, "What can't be said can't be said, and it can't be whistled either."

Thank you for not whistling it.

THE GREAT FOOL

Much of what you say makes no sense to me.

Often it makes no sense to me, either. It's foolishness offered by The Great Fool, who can't even speak. Either it rings true, or it doesn't.

The Great Fool?

Would you like to meet him?

Uh… I guess so.

Walk up to the mirror and pull your shirt over your head. Press the end of the shirt against the mirror so that you've made a sort of tunnel between you and the mirror. Go ahead….

Stand in front of the mirror and pull my shirt over my head?

Why not? What have you got to lose, but a little pride?

Okay, okay.

Good. Now, look at the face in the mirror. That's who you think you are: solid, fleshy, the mind lurking somewhere inside that object called a head with its numerous features you deem unique to you. Study it for a moment, and then reverse your attention and look back at your end of the tunnel, and tell me what you see. Take your time.

Okay... That end I'm used to. But at this end I don't see anything.

And at which end are you located?

Oh! Well, I'm at this end. But the face in the mirror is me, is a reflection of me, so....

Take for truth exactly what you see, not what you learned as a child when others told you what you were *for them*. This is about what you are *for you*. Yes, the image in the mirror is a reflection, but are you a reflection? What the mirror holds is your appearance at that distance from you, the same appearance a camera or anyone observing you from that distance would record. But you are not out there, you are here, and what you see here is what you are.

But I see nothing.

When I look back at what is looking, I see nothing also. But it's more than just a plain old nothing, isn't it? It's empty, but it's wide awake, illumined as if from within. It's empty, and yet everything in the scene – the scene itself – fits within it, occurs within it, and in that sense, is it. It is, as you say, nothing, but it's certainly a nothing unlike any imaginable, and even more remarkably, it's obviously who I am.

And this nothing is what you're calling The Great Fool?

No doubt – but then, you might take second place, standing there in front of that mirror with your shirt over your head!

Funny guy.

Okay. You saw which end of the tunnel is your end, and once you've seen what you are and where you are, you no longer need the device; you need only look in the right direction, anytime, anywhere. So, now that you're acquainted with who you are, tell me what it's like being The Great Fool.

Well – I don't know!

Yes. I don't know either. A Korean Zen master once wrote an entire book on that very subject, which he entitled *Only Don't Know*.

But, I mean, all these years I thought I was this person, this body. I just don't know about this Great Fool, this conscious nothing, if that's what I am.

Well, you *saw* what you are, and if you can't *describe* what you are, that's perfectly understandable because there's nothing there to describe. It really is the most delicious of mysteries, this nothing at the core of everything. It's a fool because it doesn't know what it is – because it's the Knower. It's a fool because pure subjectivity can never objectify itself. It's a fool because it can never do or be anything other than what it is. Love, Grace, Joy, Beatitude are some of its many names, but Laughter seems more fitting, don't you think?

But even if I understand I'm nothing filled with everything, I'm so used to being this particular part that I can't think of myself in any other way.

That's true of almost everyone, and the way it should be – because it is. However, realizing what you really are is not only a matter of understanding or of thinking about yourself in a new way. It's about profoundly *seeing* what you are, which is prior to understanding, prior to thought. It happens outside of time, is via the senses but is not sensed by any*one*, occurs as a flash of *in*sight, a wordless and thought-less seeing/knowing that may or may not be filled in later with such time-based conceptual structures as "understanding" or "believing."

But suppose I don't want to realize what I am? Suppose I'm content being who I've been all my life?

Who you *thought* you were.

Yeah. I mean, I'm doing okay, for the most part.

First, you don't have a choice as to whether or not you realize your true nature. It happens, or it doesn't. Second, it's a matter of truth for truth's sake, versus living a lie. And third, there's the little matter of life and death: as this awake nothing, there's nothing to be born or to die; as who you think you are, the grave awaits. But of course, the good news is that you are timelessly what you really are anyway – you can't be otherwise, despite what you think – so not to worry.

Well, if I'm not living as who I think I am, then who or what is doing all this business I'm calling my life?

No one is. What you call a "life" – all the memories, all that has been learned and stored away in that complex cellular apparatus called a brain, the expectations for the future, everything you can think or visualize about the universe and anything in it – all of it occurs within the empty awareness that you are. On the one hand, there is no "you" other than a tangle of thoughts/beliefs/stories appearing in this empty awareness – this "person" called "you" and this "life" you think you're living are nothing more than appearances, like all the other appearances coming and going in empty awareness. On the other hand, you are not simply nothing. As empty awareness, you are simultaneously all that appears within empty awareness, so that you are said to be Nothing/

Everything. That is to say, No-thing appears as anything and everything. They are not separate.

In that case, since this nothing appears as everything, how can you call it the Fool?

Ah, but remember, I said *Great* Fool! It's a Fool because it doesn't know what it is or how it came to be and not-be, but it's the Great Fool because it's all that ever was or will be, amen. Its other name is God, but only when it stops laughing.

NOT AN OPTION

I feel like I'm being carried in the direction of awakening, whether or not I want it. And it's not that I don't want it, but it's also not always pleasant. Sometimes it's downright scary.

Who You Are is not an option.

That's what I mean! I want it to be an option! The idea of not having any control over my life is bad enough, but worse is this idea of being no one and going on and on forever on this ride into infinity.

Once, a long time ago when I took a particularly strong dose of LSD, and having descended into a state of non-reality that I later described as "nothing but molecules," I somehow managed to say the same thing you just said about having no control and going on and on forever in a state of panic. A young hippie, a true acid-head who was with me and who was every bit as stoned as I was, said to me from a thousand miles across the room, as if he were the voice of God: "This is what you paid for, dude."

And did that help?

Hell, no. It made it worse. Not only was I condemned to eternal damnation, I had paid for it! Both in coin and in my rock-solid belief in my precious self.

And did the fear continue?

No doubt. I was a pot smoker, but soon gave it up because

of flashbacks induced by the pot. I gave up all drugs, even antihistamines, for the same reason. Eventually I began drinking heavily, and distracting myself in a hundred other destructive ways.

How did the fear surface for you? I'm curious because it seems to manifest for me as a general uneasiness, along with these occasional panic attacks about going insane.

Yes, insanity was high on my fear list. But specifically it manifested as fear over the fact that I couldn't stop hearing. I realized there was nothing in the world I could do about it, and this loss of control frightened me to the core.

What did you do to get rid of it?

Nothing. It surfaced on its own, hung around for years, then slowly dissipated. I've heard that some never experience fear, while others sink into depression, and still others lapse into fits of ecstasy. The point is, these are all experiences, and as such, are attached to the idea of personal selfhood. Glimpses beyond the self are accompanied by everything from panic to intense relief, but these reactions are not to be confused with awakening itself.

But everybody has this vision of the enlightened master glowing with bliss. You know, wearing robes and sitting in the lotus position, smiling beatifically.

Yes, that's nonsense. Awakening has nothing to do with anything, and produces no specific effects. Whatever appears appears.

So the bum on the corner could be enlightened, or a truck driver, or the CEO of General Motors?

Trungpa Rinpoche is reported to have said with regard to hidden enlightened ones: "You know who you are!" Tongue in cheek, no doubt, for he knew without question that enlightenment meant the absence of anyone to be enlightened.

Do you meditate, and have you read a lot of spiritual books or gone to see a spiritual leader?

I meditated daily for nearly ten years, sometimes twice daily, but rarely for more than a half-hour. As for books, yes, I've read many, and no, I've never gone to see a spiritual leader.

So after all those years of meditating and reading, would you say you're enlightened?

Good heavens, no! As an individual, at best I'm a fraud. I don't know where these spoken words come from, but this "life" I'm apparently living seems rarely to be in accord with them, or with any so-called "spiritual" path. Honestly, I don't know what the hell is going on, and I seem to know less every year.

But you appear so certain about this Clarity, as you sometimes refer to it. Enthusiastic, even.

Yes, it's the only sure thing, being no-thing. I've no doubt about what I really am.

Which is?

I don't know. I can perhaps tell you what I'm not, but there's no way to describe what I am, except to allude to it with words such as Clarity, Empty Awareness, The Absolute. I am absolutely one-hundred-percent certain it is All That Is, but I can't tell you what that is, except to say it is nothing and everything, the immediate form of which is This, exactly as it appears.

That makes no sense.

I agree. It's something you have to see for yourself. Hearing it from someone else is like walking into a restaurant, reading the menu, and walking out. To know what the food is like, you have to taste it yourself.

Then can you help me with this fear? Is there something I can do?

Years ago I wrote a spiritual teacher and asked him a similar question. He wrote back and said to sit with it, embrace it, watch it.

And did that work?

I never had the chance to find out because the fear didn't return, but I've sat with other emotions, and it's not that they suddenly disappear or that they fundamentally change; rather, they come and go as they please. Perhaps the lesson is that, along with the thoughts that accompany them and the things they are attached to – such as the idea of being a separate self – they are not who you are.

So it all comes down to this idea of a personal ego, again and again.

That appears to be the case. The joke is that no matter what the thoughts, no matter how great the struggle to be or not to be whatever you think you are, you can never be disconnected from This. It's not possible. And every attempt to do so, every act designed to maintain the falsehood, results in one or another form of stress, most of it buried or ignored or considered "normal," but occasionally crashing into con-sciousness as depression or rage or panic. Eventually, though, with Clarity, our pitiful attempts to be what we can never be are seen as just that – pitiful. Or perhaps hilarious. All part of the Great Hoax.

So we're back to that: Who I Am is not an option.

Not an option. And we've never left it.

SPACE AND TIME

I've read a couple of books about being in the here and now, and it makes sense to me because if I'm lost in thoughts of being elsewhere in the past or future, I'm really not living my life.

I use the terms "here' and "now" in our conversations mostly to point to This, What We Are. But really there is no here and now, as opposed to there and then. Used correctly, in a certain context, words can reveal the nonexistence of what they popularly stand for, and thereby open the door to a glimpse of the truth.

So you see no value in living a mindful life in the here and now?

The idea of living your life in the here and now is no better than living it in the there and then, the problem being that you still think you are a separate "you" living a "life." From the point of view of a separate self, I suppose there are degrees of nonsense, but really, nonsense is just nonsense.

Are you saying there is no time?

There is the *appearance* of time, but What We Are is timeless. We are No-time appearing as time. Nothing could appear unless it could "last." But to answer your question: No, there is no such thing as time.

But we're here in the present moment, having this conversation.

What people believe is the present moment is actually the past. You could think of it as projected, and therefore on its way out, from the nearest and briefest flicker of a subatomic particle to the remotest galaxy. Or take science's story, that light reflected off an object, even one as close as that pencil, takes time to reach your eyes, be converted into electro-chemical signals, and subsequently pass to the brain where perception occurs. So that, in effect, you are living in the past. Or perhaps you are living in the future, but don't yet know it. According to this story, the past is gone, the future hasn't dawned on you yet, and what you consider the present has already passed.

But I'm talking to you. I'm doing this now, not then. If I weren't here and weren't talking to you now, this "present" wouldn't be happening!

We think we influence the present moment, but even "we" are in the past! It all happens without the least bit of input from what we think of as our "selves," since what we think of as our "selves" has already happened, is "out there" in the "past." So, using this logic, why be concerned about any-thing? There's nothing that can be done about it because it's already over. Perhaps the only reason you think you influ-ence what appears is because you're everything that ever appeared or will appear, all at once. Recognizing this, you are nearing the truth.

Wait. Let's go back to the subject of time....

And space.

Okay, space-time, because they are intertwined....

In such a way that, from the point of view of an observer, the farther away an object appears in space, the further back it is in time. This is the mechanism of appearance – it's how I manifest as the world, and it is also science's story. But it's not real.

What do you mean, it's not real? You're sitting in this room. Space-time is all around you. It's what you're in!

On the contrary, space-time is in Me. Space-time is what I am in manifestation, and I am infinitely deep and always Here. So you see, you have it backwards.

I don't know, it seems perfectly real and "out there" to me.

I alone am real, and I am No-thing. Space-time is the mechanism whereby I dream the universe. I am the sole Dreamer, and the universe is my dream. Space-time is What I Am because I am dreaming it, but it is only a dream. Anyone can say this, because the center of the universe is everywhere, and is always seen as Here. Does that help?

A little, but it's so completely backwards from what I'm used to, not to mention that it makes a mockery of the way we view the universe and everything in it.

As self-existing and "real" and separate from What We Are, yes, that way of viewing the universe is the Great Joke, and we've played it on ourselves. Seen correctly, though, it is seen as perfect, and what better way to see anything, never mind everything? Seen correctly, it is also seen as Real, in that it is What We Are, which is pure non-dual Subjectivity.

You said that space-time is in you. I can say that also?

Not only say it, you can *see* it. Look back at what is looking. Attend to This Which You Are. Notice how empty and how huge you are, so that everything, no matter what the scene, fits easily within. Wherever you look, space-time is *inside* you.

I don't think I'm empty, and I certainly don't feel huge.

This isn't about thinking or feeling. It's about pure looking, prior to thought. Take off your glasses and hold them out in front of you. Go ahead....
      Now bring them in slowly, and watch them carefully.... Closer.... Slowly.... And put them on.
      Tell me what happened.

The glasses became a monocle. It's like I have one eye instead of two.

Describe that eye.

It's just one big eye – yes, I see what you mean, it really is huge, if you take the whole thing to be an eye. But of course, it isn't, is it?

Take what you see as evidence, not what you assume, not what you learned from others.

Well, what I see is one enormous eye, but it's not really an eye, it's like this huge oval nothing.

Is it aware?

Yes, definitely.

Is it empty?

Yes.

And is it also filled to the brim with the scene?

Yes, including the monocle in front, my arms...and when I look down, even my body.

So your body, the room and the objects in it are in *you* – not the other way around. Has it *ever* been the other way, the way you were taught, the way you assumed it was?

No, I guess it hasn't.

So you see, all of space-time is in you. It *can't* be any other way.

But if I look at that coffee cup on the desk, I see it as over there, not inside me.

Yes, that's the way you've been conditioned to view yourself and the objects of the world – as separate, with you in a body over here and everything else out there. However, you are not in a body, any more than you are in that cup or desk. Look: coffee cup, awareness of coffee cup – how are they separate? Would you say awareness is in the coffee cup, or the coffee cup is in awareness?

Definitely the latter.

Because awareness is no-thing and is therefore capacity for everything, and in that way is not separate from what it is capacity for.

And I am *my awareness?*

Yes, but this is not a personal awareness among other personal awarenesses. There is only awareness. Since awareness is no-thing, how could there be multiple or different awarenesses? There's nothing to be different or multiple! When you look Here, when you realize what you are, you see that the coffee cup and awareness are the same. And ultimately, they are no-thing, and in that lies their absolute reality. *Your* absolute reality.

Why do you say they are both no-thing?

The answer that comes to mind is that the coffee cup could not exist without awareness, but awareness exists without the coffee cup.

So would you suggest I use my glasses when I want to see in this way?

No, of course not. Using your glasses is simply another device to direct your attention away from objects "out there" and bring it "back here" to what you really are. Now that you know where to look, you no longer need the device, unless you find it helpful. Incidentally, this looking at what is looking doesn't preclude the seeing of objects or from carrying on as you normally would with any activity. It is looking here *and* there at the same time, or two-way looking, but primarily attending to this empty Capacity and noticing what fills it. This can be done anytime, anywhere – during which you might just realize that both are always Here and always Now.

Because all of space-time is in Me.

Yes. It's called Presence, and it's all that is.

CONTROL

You mentioned previously that you experienced loss-of-control problems after your LSD sessions, and that this evoked fear, and even panic. Rather than have fear surprise me, I'd rather work with control issues beforehand so that I'm not overwhelmed.

So you want to control your loss-of-control issues on the so-called path to awakening?

I guess you could put it that way. I'd rather not come unglued, as they say.

Well, good luck, because whether or not you realize it, you were never glued. Let me add, however, that not everyone experiences fear. Some experience joy or relief, even ecstasy – but all of these experiences are part of manifestation, and what you are is prior to that. The fact remains, as who you think you are, you have no control over anything, and as who you really are – Awake No-thing – you *are* everything, so the question of control is not an issue.

I don't see it like that. Sure, there are things I can't control, like the weather, but when it comes to this body and mind, I'm in charge. It's just so obvious.

It may seem that way, but it's not the case. Try this: Close your eyes, sit back and relax... Now let your attention fall on the sounds you hear – the fan, voices in the distance, a radio – and notice that you hear them right where you are and nowhere else. Now place your fingers in your ears to block out the sounds, and notice that you can still hear – hear a hum, maybe, hear your fingers moving a little, hear stray sounds coming through. Now try to *stop* hearing – and notice that you can't.

Next, still with eyes closed, attend to the pressures you feel sitting on that chair, your feet on the floor, your hands in your lap, the air on your skin. Focus on these feelings, for a minute, then try to *stop* feeling them, and notice you can't. No matter what you're doing, you can't stop feeling. Even if you were suspended in a tank of warm salt water, you'd still feel something.

Now open your eyes and attend to the scene. Close them again and notice you can't stop seeing – you may not see objects, but you still see, even if it's the inside of your eyelids.

So how is it that you are in charge of your body if you can't even stop your hearing, your feeling, your seeing? How is it that they go on without you, no matter what you do about it? You say, "But I'll go to sleep." And do you do that? You lie down, but do you have any control over the moment of going to sleep? Rather, doesn't sleep just happen to you? And anyway, during sleep, do you really stop hearing or feeling or seeing? What about dreams? And how is it that a sound or a light can wake you up?

The fact is, you have no control because this "you" is fictitious. Control of anything by a "you" is an illusion. The truth is that what you really are is the hearing, the feeling, the seeing, all going on without a "you." You are pure awareness and everything appearing within it – the sounds, the feelings, the sights. There is no seer here and something seen over there. They are one and the same – and not even that.

Yes, but who closed my eyes and relaxed? I did! Who noticed their hearing and feeling and seeing? I did! You yourself confirmed it with your instructions when you told me to do this or that.

From the point of view of First-Person-Singular, which is All That Is, no one told anyone to do those things, but we converse in conventional terms or cannot converse at all, despite the fact that we are conversing as though in a dream. All language is like this; it is dualistic by nature, and although language can never reveal what you are, if used correctly it can at least point in the right direction. "You" didn't close your eyes and relax, nor did "you" do anything else. It appeared to happen, as everything else appears to happen. And it all happens as First-Person-Singular. First-Person-Singular is the movement, so you say "I" did it, but mistakenly believe that the "I" is a separate self.

So there's no "you" telling me to do those things?

No. It just appears. How can I do something when What I Am is no-thing. Or how can I do something when I'm everything? Take the individual "I" out of it, and it just *is*.

This isn't helping me get a handle on my control issues. It feels more like I shouldn't be having this conversation with you.

You *should* be having it because it's appearing. It's obviously time, or it wouldn't be happening.

What will become of me? I have visions of going mad, of being terminally depressed. I can't stand the thought of losing every-thing I've built for myself, losing my family and friends and possessions and just going with whatever happens minute by minute like some dummy. Don't you ever stand up for yourself and for what you believe in?

No.

But you seem to function like everyone else.

Maybe so, but as Who I Really Am I don't "believe in" or stand up" for anything because I am all things.

You just let people walk all over you?

This appearance you refer to will say "no" just as easily as it will say "yes" – it all depends on circumstances and conditioning. You're confusing the body with who I am. What you see here is an appearance, lent form by distance.

Then where are you?

I'm not, and neither are you. We can both say it, not as "we," but as "I" – "I am, and I am not."

I don't understand. It seems to me that if you're nobody, as you say, you're just a dust mote in the wind. Anyone can take advantage of you.

The opposite is true. What I am is immutable, and everything passes through me. Nothing can take advantage of me because I appear as everything. I am No-thing filled with all things, so what could take advantage of what? I am both totally vulnerable and totally invulnerable.

Ah! So you admit that you're vulnerable!

Completely. As this clear open space, I have nothing with which to keep you or anything else out. I *can't* resist you – I may try, but it's not possible, because there's nothing here to resist you with. This is also a description of true intimacy, of love. No doubt it is the meaning of Jesus's "dying so that others may live in me." You are my life, and all that happens, happens in Me – how much more vulnerable could I be?

Then how could you be invulnerable?

I've already said it – nothing can take advantage of me because I appear as everything. This is not philosophy; these are not idle words tossed around for intellectual stimulation; this is simplicity itself, easily seen in an instant. Look *within*. Look back at what is looking, attend to what is attending, and see – actually *see* – no face, no head, nothing but luminous empty space, wide open and vibrantly aware. It's like looking out of a window with no frame and no glass. This is what you *are*, and within it – wedded to it – appears the moment-by-moment changing scene, the whole vast array we call the "world." Totally vulnerable, you are totally invulnerable.

Just now as you were saying that, I looked back, and it sent shivers through my body.

I noticed.

But it wasn't exactly fear that I felt. I don't know what it was, really, but it had to do with actually looking, *instead of trying to figure all this out.*

Yes. Looking is the key.

I mean, I know there's a face and a head here – but knowing isn't the same as looking, is it?

No, it isn't. Knowing is what you learned from others. Knowing is thought, and is mediate. Looking is immediate, unmediated, prior to thought. Looking at what is looking is looking looking at itself, and is instantaneous, or rather, timeless. You've *learned* that that object over there is a "tree" and those are "buildings" and both are part of a world "out there," while you are in a body "over here." You've *learned* that they are objects, and because others have told you what you are for them, which is an object, you've learned that *you* are an object, an individual self. So you say, "I" am "me" – as if there were two of you! You've diminished yourself. Believing what you've been told, replacing direct seeing with the language of objects, you *think* you're a third-person, when instead you can *see* you are First-Person-Singular. You've learned from others, and now firmly believe that you are a tiny speck in an infinite universe, when just the opposite is plainly on view. All you need is to look.

So that what we're talking about here, this First-Person-Singular view, isn't about losing control, it's about gaining control.

In a manner of speaking, yes, except it's not about gaining anything, it's about discovering what you already are. At the level of the absolute, zero control and total control, like all opposites, are the same. And not the same as "equal" or "one," but as "not an issue." There is no "you" to have or not have control, and there is nothing separate from you over which you could have or not have control.

The point is moot.

Always.

THE WHOLE ENCHILADA

You showed me the pointing exercise, and I see this Emptiness here, maybe more than I want to. My question today is: After you see No-thing, what then?

What then?

Yes. It's like I see it, but so what?

Oh. Well, it's no big deal. It's just that *you're god, and the whole freaking universe is inside you!*

Jeez, you don't have to yell at me.

[*The next day*]

I'm still having a problem with this No-thing thing.

What sort of problem?

Well, it's like I want to...[suddenly leaps into the air, twists, and lands facing in the opposite direction]...*catch it in the act!*

Ha!

I want to find it, you know? Touch it.

But it's *nothing!*

Yes, and that scares me a little.

There's nothing here to scare you, and anyway, who's scaring whom?

You mean there's nobody here to scare?

And nobody doing the scaring. Fear arises because of a false belief that what you are is a separate self, and as you can see, that's not what you are. You are No-thing appearing as Everything. As No-thing, what's to scare? As Everything, how could there be something apart to scare something else? You're the entire shebang, my friend. The whole enchilada.

You've got a point there. You've got a point.

Yes, and the points are worthless unless you see for yourself. Look, and be This Which You Are.

THE ONE THOUGHT

I can't get past my thinking. What I mean is, I'm convinced I'm my thinking—I can't see any difference between awareness and thinking. I'm a mind, and proof of that is that I think.

You think you're a mind, and proof of that is that you think you're a mind? Where is the "you" in that?

The process itself. The thinking.

Sounds like an infinite regression to me, but if you say so, so be it.

What do you think I am?

Not thinking, for sure.

Then what?

You are Nothing, and Nothing cannot think about any-thing except as Everything thinking about anything, and when Everything thinks about Itself, it thinks *The One Thought*—which is beyond all thinking.

I don't know what you just said, and I don't know whether I should be thankful or sorry I asked the question!

Be neither. Look within. *See* what you are. If you tell me you're Seeing seeing Seeing—which is nothing, or No-*thing*—you win the prize. If you say you think you're thinking, you haven't seen, and although you still win the

116

prize, you don't know it.

So what is thought? Obviously it's personal, since only I can have these thoughts, these memories, and so on.

It's personal and it's not personal. You are Absolute Nothing, empty and clear of the least speck of anything, and because you are Absolute Nothing, you are room for anything whatsoever. The distinction I make between nothing nothing and Absolute Nothing is that nothing is just nothing, the opposite of something, whereas Absolute Nothing, because it is absolute, is also Everything; furthermore, Absolute Nothing is *aware* it is Absolute Nothing-Everything. You can picture Absolute Nothing as *Capacity* for everything – the one silent, immutable, awake; the other all that appears and disappears within it, which is the world. The one transcendent, the other immanent. The one Spirit, the other Body – as One.

As Absolute Nothing, you are prior to thoughts, you are aware of thoughts. As Absolute Nothing, where you are – which is always Here – there is nothing to think *with*, so how could thoughts be personal? Alternatively, since you are all that appears – and all that appears includes thoughts – thoughts are entirely personal. After all, there is no one else to think them! Only God thinks, and you cannot be separate from God.

The point is, thoughts are not "yours" as an individual, a separate self. Thoughts are attached to the "things" of this world, *are*, in fact, this world. Thoughts make up your belief that you are a separate self, housed in a body, having a mind. How else could thought explain itself in such a context without presuming the existence of a mind? What is mind? All this conceptual activity is downstream of What You Are, is secondary to primary Truth.

And thinking this is The One Thought?

I would say *seeing* this is The One Thought. Seeing and being are the same, when it comes to The One Thought.

FULFILLMENT

I've never understood what it means to be fulfilled.

Right. It's a strange word, fulfillment. I don't think anyone knows what it means. When they get what they think they want, they want more, and fulfillment always seems to be just out of reach.

With me, it's a case of not knowing where to begin. There's a yearning for something, but I don't know what. So I buy this or that, or join clubs, or meet new people, but underneath it all, the yearning persists.

I think it has to do with an intuitive knowledge of what we really are, which is Pure Emptiness. Deep down we know this, but to the ego it feels like a hole at the core of our being, one that is perceived as a defect, a fault, and one that we must somehow fill. Relationships, power, money, fame – or as they say: sex, drugs, and rock and roll – are some of the ways we attempt to fill that hole, but of course it turns out to be bottomless and we never succeed.

Which is why we don't understand the meaning of fulfillment?

Yes. The irony is that right now we are so filled to the brim that there isn't room for one iota of anything more. We are *always* fulfilled – which is another reason we don't understand the meaning of the term – there's nothing to get that would change how filled we already are!

You are referring, I assume, to the "pointing exercise", seeing that I am totally empty and yet totally filled with the scene.

Yes. Looking back, and especially when you spread your arms and hold this awake and empty Eye that you are, it's obvious that you are Capacity for the scene that fills it. Not partially fills it, but totally. Every time you look.

But the Emptiness is there as well. It doesn't vanish because it's filled with the scene.

Correct. Without Emptiness, there would be no filling. Without Emptiness, there would be no *scene*. It's crucial to see that they are not two. That is, Emptiness and the scene that appears in it are not separate. It is equally crucial to attend primarily to Emptiness. We are accustomed to attending to the scene only, and this is the cause of our pervasive sense of lack. We're missing ourselves, What We Really Are. We feel the Emptiness at our core, but avoid it, deny it, call it an "issue" and try to fill it—with more and different scenery, of course. The truth is, the Emptiness at our core is not a fault. It's divine! It's Divinity Itself, and it's Who We Are. So, you see, the idea of fulfillment is absurd.

And yet, after this conversation, and looking Here, I'm fulfilled!

Yes, that's the way of it also.

Really, all I need do is look Here.

Yes. Look Here, and get "there" thrown in in the bargain.

SHADOW BOXING

I'm miserable.

I can see that.

Everything pisses me off, it seems. It's just so unfair. I shouldn't be here, you know. I don't deserve this.

Really! What do you deserve?

Well, not this! My family's disowned me, I'm locked up for something I didn't do, I'm surrounded by idiots!

Thanks!

Not you. Everyone else. But even you piss me off sometimes, because none of this madness seems to bother you.

And it should?

Right. You're in prison, man. Take a look around!

I have, and I don't see it that way. Prison is in me.

Meaning?

Meaning that the difference between you and me is that you're battling who you are, and I'm not. You think you're pissed off at "them," you think "it" is unfair, you think you don't deserve "this," but it's all you! How could it be unfair? How could you not deserve what you *are*? The world is your reflection, and closer than that.

So you're laying this on me. I'm the one to blame for this mess.

In a manner of speaking, yes. But I wouldn't use the word "blame," and it's not a mess, it's more beautiful and amazing than you can imagine.

I heard that your son died a few years back. You call that beautiful and amazing? Did you even grieve for him?

I did, at first. But then I came to see that he didn't die, because he was me. Thinking he was gone, thinking he shouldn't have died, thinking I wasn't there for him when I should have been, thinking I'd miss him, were all part of a tale of separation that I alone was spinning. And all along, he was Who I Am.

It sounds to me like you just laid down and let life walk all over you, like you gave up. That's no way to live, man.

It's just the opposite. Life keeps showing up, and it's all Who I Am, all marvelously orchestrated by Who I Am. It's the *only* way to live. The alternative is to believe the painful thoughts that come, or what others tell me I am – which is no life at all, and leads only to death.

So you have no problems?

No. I think it was Lennon who sang, "There are no problems, only solutions."

You never feel pain, or sadness, or desire?

I do, but I don't believe the thoughts behind them, so these feelings come in, hang around for their allotted span, and move out. Often they're a blessing because they serve as taps on the shoulder, reminders of Clarity.

So what happens if you get a cellmate who plays his radio super-loud all day long?

I won't know until it happens. I may listen to it, I may use earplugs, I may ask him to turn it off. But nowhere is there a "should" or "shouldn't." Expectations are not only painful when they are not met, they're ridiculous to hold in the first place. Having expectations is moving away from yourself. Seeking anything other than what is, is denying what you are.

Well, I'd never let someone disrespect me like that. I expect things, I try things, and I know how things should be. You've lost hope, man.

Yes, I have, and thank goodness! Hope is absurd. And don't get me wrong, I'm not saying you shouldn't have hope or shouldn't believe what you believe or live as you live – this too is perfect, exactly as it is.

Yeah, some of us have to just suck it up and keep fighting, you know?

Yes. As long as you don't mind shadow boxing. And losing.

EVERYTHING MATTERS

You've said that for a long time in your life you held the attitude that nothing matters, but that now it's just the opposite.

Yes. Everything matters.

How did you switch from one to the other?

It's difficult to explain. It's not something I chose to do. I would say it's the result of a new way of looking, but even that sounds deliberate. It's a flip, a metanoesis, and it seems to happen as a result of seeing your true nature, but it's not willed; it's automatic and concurrent with the seeing; it comes from the seeing but also *is* the seeing.

Prior to this flip, would you say your outlook was nihilistic, and when did that begin?

Yes, I suppose it was nihilistic, and it began when I was a child, based primarily on the idea that there was something wrong with me and that I would never amount to anything. I could say I learned these beliefs from others early on, but it goes deeper than that. There really *was* something wrong – I was growing down, not up, contracting from childlike open-ness into the lie of a separate self. The irony is that I would never amount to anything because I was never anything and always everything to begin with!

Do you think this contraction was the reason you later fell into crime?

Yes, but only because I fell to the extreme. The great majority of people don't fall into crime, despite having contracted into separate selves in what we consider the "normal" process of maturing. They may experience a sense of angst, but most manage to distract themselves with families and careers, sports, shopping, the artifacts of culture and religion. Why I went to the lowest point, I don't know, but it would eventually lead to the gates of heaven.

Going down, not up?

Oh yes. Down with Dante Alighieri into the pits of hell, and *through* to the heavenly realms.

Would you recommend that as a path?

Oh hell no! Let me reiterate, waking up isn't something you *do*. Even *thinking* that the path to heaven involves harming oneself and others is ludicrous.

All paths are ludicrous, according to you.

Yes. Someone once said, "There is no path from here to here." But at least those other paths are politically correct!

You're joking.

Yes.

Well, then, let me ask you again about "nothing matters." When you first mentioned it, I actually thought you were referring to "Emptiness." There's a double entendre there, you know.

Yes. *Nothing* matters. It's interesting that you mention that because that happened also, although many years later, and after I had tried LSD and stuck my toes in the Zen pool, so to speak. Nothingness, Emptiness, became prominent, in that I identified with it on a deeper level and believed it was the core of my being, the very being of the universe. And guess what? Nothing changed, in terms of my outlook!

I was still this limited separate self, still seeing myself and others as objects, and now with an even greater sense of hollowness at my center, a gaping hole of gigantic proportions, never to be filled.

So much for Nirvana.

Yes. Emptiness is a trap not to get caught in, but as I said, it's also a trap door.

So did you fall through the trap door all at once, and were you free from then on?

No, it's not like that. The trap door, the flip, is always here. It happens, but the idea of permanence, or of being permanently awake, is not it. Time is not a factor in it.

So it's sudden, but not permanent.

Yes, I suppose you could say that, although that's not quite accurate either. In some, the *experience*, or the *appearance*, of permanence may occur.

And what was it that opened the door?

The difference was between thinking and seeing, between conceptualizing and apprehending. When you actually see what you are, you realize you are not simply nothing, but Absolute Nothing, which is also Everything. When this happens, the limited separate self is transformed into the All Self, and gratitude pours out. Suddenly everything matters, and how!

Because it's what you are?

Yes, but beyond that. Beyond "you" and "are." Beyond words altogether.

This downward path of Dante's that led eventually to heaven, can you say more about that?

No, because I'm not a scholar of *The Divine Comedy*, and there's no need to get into a lengthy discussion. It can, however, be seen – actually physically seen – if you'd like to try.

I'd like.

Turn your chair and face me. Straighten your legs in front of you. Now, going only on present evidence, taking for true exactly what you see, scan down from the top of my head to my feet, then to your feet and down to your chest – and notice that I am right-side-up, whereas you are upside down.

So I am!

Okay, let me get out the way so you can see out the window. Now look at the sky, then slowly drop your gaze to the mountains below, down farther now to the mesas and trees and the fences...on down to the windowsill, the wall inside, the floor...now down to your feet, *down* to your knees, your thighs, down further to your abdomen, chest, all way down to the bottom of the world and – what?

It ends at my chest.

Fall through. Actually look at what is given below your chest, what is at the bottom, the Ground of absolutely everything that is "up there." Go on – all the way down...

Oh! It's the pointing exercise. It's what I'm looking out of – Empty Awareness.

Exactly. Now, *while still attending to Empty Awareness,* allow your gaze to slowly rise, up to your chest, abdomen, legs, the room, trees, mountains, and sky. What you are is not merely Empty Awareness but Empty Awareness filled with the scene, one and the same. From the very depths springs the entire universe, yet all of it within. What you are is the Ground, and all that it is Ground for.

That's amazing! It's literal!

Yes. It's a metaphor only when you're stuck in who you think you are. When you see what you really are, it's literal. And then the notion of a "you" as a separate self is no longer in question.

This has to be seen, it can't be told. And for some reason, this time it seemed more powerful than the pointing exercise was for me.

The meaning of it, the realization that goes along with it and that is downstream of the actual seeing may be more powerful, but the seeing itself is always the same, prior to any thoughts or feelings about it. It's really very matter-of-fact, which of course it has to be because Empty Awareness never changes. It is always what it is because it is timeless.

Why don't seekers go around pointing at themselves? It's so easy. Talk about a picture being worth a thousand words!

A friend distinguishes between the Word and the Vision by pointing out that the Word has been around for five thousand years or more, and now we've been introduced to the Vision, that which the word "in-sight" truly means: actually physically *looking* at This.

The Word versus the Vision.

Yes. All along, the masters of different traditions have been saying it, to *look* within. Not to talk or write about within, but to look. The Word may lead you to the gate, but only the Vision will open it. In the beginning was the Word, in the end the Vision.

The Beatific Vision of Beatrice?

Yes.

But why hasn't this Vision thing caught on? If it's so easy and so direct, why don't more people see it for themselves?

Because it's so easy and so direct! It's right in front of the nose they don't have, so nobody can find it. It's too innocent, too unsophisticated, too near and too clear. It's in the opposite direction from where they normally look. And it's perceived, or mis-perceived, as the end of the separate self, the end of the world as they know it. "End of story," as they say.

So they're afraid of dying.

Worse than dying. At least with death comes the possibility of another life or an afterlife. But with the Vision, which is prior to the concepts of birth and death or any other experience by a self, everything ends. The irony is, the fear of dissolution is unfounded because not only do they discover they are Nothing, they also discover they are Everything. The Beatific vision is not a vision of hell, but of heaven.

Terrifying just the same, considering what is lost.

Nothing is lost! That's the Great Joke, the Cosmic Hoax. Have a look, and have a laugh! It's simply a case of misplaced identity, a misapprehension, a fiction innocently told because it was told to you and told to the one before you.

So it's a matter of facing in the right direction, and facing it. Or should I say, no-facing it?

Yes, no-facing it. There's no face and nothing separate to face, is there? It's so easy, it's a wonder everyone doesn't see it. It's what they are, and what could be easier than being what they are?

These "devices," as you call them – where did you get the idea for them?

From Douglas Harding and his friends.

Oh yes, I've heard of him. He wrote On Having No Head, *as I remember.*

And several other books. His message, sometimes referred to as "The Headless Way," is the fast track Home, particularly suited to the Western temperament because it's down-to-earth, scientific, and requires simply that you look for yourself, rather than believe what you hear from others. You can spend ten thousand lifetimes reading and listening to the words of the spiritual masters and not see what you see in a flash of genuine insight.

But these devices are so ridiculously unholy. I mean, come on! A sheet of cardboard with a hole in it, a pointing finger?

There's nothing holy about what you are. You want to put on robes and sniff incense all day, be my guest. You want to see what you are, then forget all that and do something ridiculous. These devices are no more than that – devices. They coax you into turning within. They drag your attention away from objects "out there" and direct it instead to what is attending, to what you are, where you are.

Why do you say it's scientific?

Because, in the spirit of science, the directive is to take for truth exactly what is presented, not what is assumed or imagined.

That's what I want to talk to you about today. You've said that I'm not what I think I am, a separate self. But this overwhelming sense of being here, this feeling of "I am," can't be dismissed. I don't imagine this, I don't think my way into it, it's really here, and it's me – I can't deny it. I've read that what I really am is impersonal, but it feels about as personal as personal can get.

Yes, I agree. It's either impersonal or personal depending on where you place your identity. If you're convinced you're a limited separate self, then what you really are is said to be impersonal, because the Absolute transcends the idea of limited ego. If, however, you see that what you are is the Absolute, then what you are is personal, because All That Is is nothing but you.

I sometimes say I'm suprapersonal. Like you, I can't call what I am "impersonal," for above all I am Presence. I've said that the ego is not real; it is merely a string of thoughts that together define what I call "myself," this individual "me" with a particular name and form. But in another sense it is as real as anything else, and denying it only strengthens its hold. This sense of Presence, this I Am that emanates from the Awake Empty Core of this solitary "I," is the true ground of what we each surmise to be a separate ego, which is simply a miniature and misplaced version of the One True Presence, so that we need not discard it (as if it could!), we need only to see through the boundaries – boundaries that were not truly there to begin with – and watch it fly to the limit, so that Presence becomes what it always was, which is All That Is. I Am is another of my names, and I am *everything.*

How do I go about removing the fictitious boundaries, then? Why does this ego self have to happen, anyway? Why can't we just be what we really are?

There's no answer to these questions. "How?" and "Why?" come from the limited point of view of a separate self, and whatever answers are supplied usually result in the main-tenance or reinforcement of that same separate self – all of which is a charade based upon a bogus premise. When you see what you really are, you see that you *never were* merely a separate self, that the Presence you recognize was applied to a tiny part of the Whole that you truly are. And since you are that Whole, the application was done by none other than what you are. So there is no answer to "Why?" And as for "How?", the best I can offer is: Look!

TO MEDITATE OR NOT TO MEDITATE

What about meditation? Do you think I should meditate?

Have you noticed that, as Pure Awareness, you can't get wet in the shower? When you touch something, do you touch it, or does it touch you? Is it, "Wherever you go, there you are," or is it rather, "I Am, no matter what shows up"? Do you ever wonder why what you believe and What Is are so often at odds?

What's any of that got to do with meditation?

Well, what's meditation got to do with any of that?

I don't know. But anyway, do you think I should meditate?

Meditation has its benefits. For instance, you may notice for the first time the quiet space between thoughts, the background that is always there, in which thoughts come and go. During the years I meditated, however, I continued to believe I *was* my thoughts; I saw no distinction between awareness and thoughts. Meditation also is helpful in stress reduction, mind-body healing, attention to detail, and other functions related to self-improvement. So you become a calmer, healthier, more attentive guy – but then one day the phone rings and your wife tells you the cat mistook your stamp collection for kitty litter, and suddenly you're planning ten ways to snuff out Fluffy's nine lives.

Do you ever give a straight answer?

Sure.

Well then, do you think I should meditate?

I don't know.

You don't recommend it, then?

I don't recommend anything because I don't see anything needed.

Well, if I decide to try meditation, will you teach me how?

I'd be happy to.

THE NEW RELIGION

You've said that science is the new religion, and that the popularity of recent books about physics and astronomy is not curiosity about science per se, but about the spiritual or mystical meaning within. What do you mean by that?

Science basically is about discovering what the world is made of and how it works; its typical method is to dismantle phenomena into ever smaller parts. Push this reduction far enough, you reach the Great Question Mark, the Emptiness at the heart of all that appears as the world, where reality as we know it breaks down, where nothing makes sense. At this frontier, how much more mystical could it get? Our interest in science is more than casual. Somebody once said that all desire is desire for God, and the same principle applies here. All searching is searching for God. Moreover, it is God searching for Himself.

God searching for Himself?

Yes. All this business, this busywork we call "world," is God appearing as Other mirroring God. It's the Great Game. How otherwise could God become aware of Himself? How could He awaken to what He is unless He pretends to fall asleep? Religion made do for awhile. And keep in mind that it was religion, specifically Christianity, that gave birth to science. And science, in order to properly do its job, had to emerge from the shell of its parent and strike out on its own. And now here we are, God knocking on his own door and discovering He's already inside!

This is crazy!

It is. It's hilarious, too.

Can you give me an example of how science leads to mysticism?

It's basic stuff, really, although most people seem to avoid the deeper meaning. Say I'm the observer scientist. You and a few objects in this room represent the world. I want to find out what you are, so I begin by examining you at this distance, and I call you a "human being," and the object you are sitting on a "chair," the object nearby a "table." To discover just what a human being is, I decide to take you apart, and to do that, I move closer, and determine that you are a constructed of parts: organs, bones, blood, and so on. Closer still, and now with magnifying instruments, I find that you are made up of even smaller parts, or "cells," each one alive in its own right – a vast city of them acting in concert – and I decide you are a swarm of billions of tiny animals, three times as many as there are humans on this planet. But now, moving still closer, I observe that these cells are made up of an even vaster number of parts called molecules – and at this point, having also examined the other objects in the room, the lines begin to blur between what I call "you" and what I call the "chair" you are supposedly sitting on, the "table" nearby and even the surrounding "air." Still closer, I find atoms, then protons and electrons and a host of other sub-atomic particles briefly appearing as "events" in mostly empty space. Now there are no things, no boundaries, no localities – there is nothing, and what remains of the world is reduced to "probabilities" of "events" relying on the presence of an observer. Here, everything I could call something is not only strange, it's basically gone!

Now – I'm sitting here and you're sitting there across from me on that chair, with this table nearby. Taking the above and applying it to our situation, what have we got?

We've got nothing we can call anything! I've examined you and the objects in this room, and I've concluded that all of it is nothing more than empty space punctuated by fleeting wisps of mysterious energy; at the level of the very small, there are only probabilities collapsing into actualities at the moment of observation. So we have you (empty space) sitting on that chair (empty space) next to this table (empty space) across from me (empty space). So what's going on here? Where is there a "me" and a "you" in this empty space?

I see your point. But what about the observer?

Ah yes, the observer. Now that's the $64,000 question! Who or where is the observer? Obviously I am the observer in our example, but what am I but empty space? So how am I different from you or any other object in the room? I am not a human being, I am not an object, I am no "thing" at all, and yet I am somehow present. The only conclusion I can possibly reach is that the observer is this very same empty space that we've described, collapsing itself into apparent actuality (in the form of the universe and everything in it). For what else is there? I am the Observer and the Observer is "I," and anyone can say it because "I" am everywhere! And I am no thing – I can see this, because I am plainly on display.

Out there, wherever I look?

As science would demonstrate, yes. But there is an easier way to see what you are, one that is readily available anytime. Really, there is no such place as "out there." Space/time itself is what is "collapsed" into apparent actuality by the observer. And who is this observer? God. And where is He? Here. Not "here" in the sense of a place versus another place, but in the sense of total presence. Turn your attention back on itself, attend to who is attending, actually look back at what you are looking out of, and "see" the luminous

Aware Emptiness that is God. It was Meister Eckhart who said, "The eyes with which I see God are the same eyes with which He sees me."

Then you and I... Then there is no "you" and "I"?

Right. There is only the Observer, aka Aware Emptiness, aka God.

It just occurred to me that this everywhere empty space revealed by science is having a conversation about itself! Doesn't that seem a little unlikely?

No more unlikely than the appearance of the universe. Or the Aware Emptiness in which it appears – how did *that* come about? There could be – there *should* be – simply nothing at all. Instead, there is this awake presence, this no-thing called God in whom I fully participate, awake not only to what appears within His scope, but awake to Himself! Out of nowhere, out of nothing, God is. And if it amazes me, imagine how it amazes Him! God stupefies Himself simply by His presence, having no idea how He pulls it off. And let me add that without this mystery of self-origination, God would not be God.

And then, after creating Himself, he creates the universe?

Yes, in the sense that this Aware Emptiness is the timeless and immutable Ground in which everything arises and passes away, but there is no "before" and "after" involved. Nor is there any separation, so you could also say that God and the universe arise together. This divine and fully awake No-thing and the universe that arises within it are not two. You cannot say they are one, because that would be misleading. They are not two, and not one, and they are also not nothing. For that matter, they are not "they." They are This

138

Which Is, which is about all that can be said about God without retreating from Him.

And I am this?

What else could you be?

I don't know. I guess I was hoping for something a little more substantial.

Like a body?

Yes. A body. A place. Living quarters, you could say.

But the whole world is your body. Why confine yourself to that appearance you call "flesh"? You are much much more than your flesh body, and as we've already seen, much much less. You are this luminous No-thing here "within," and absolutely everything that appears in its boundless presence.

But how do I appear as anything? How does appearance appear?

Via three dimensions of space and one of time, called "space-time."

And I, as what I really am, do that?

Who else is there to do anything? But let me add that it is not something *done* by someone. Nothing is done. It simply is. Itself *itselfs*, you could say. Does that make sense?

Of course not.

Good. Then we're near. The rest is up to silence.

SEEING ONE, SEEING ALL

I was walking back from the library today and looking at the buildings lit up in the morning light, the mountains beyond – just the angle of everything from where I was – and it occurred to me that no one else in the entire world had this one particular view, that it was reserved only for me. And then I remembered what you said about nothing being separate, and in that moment, it seemed the most absurd thing you'd ever said.

In what way?

We're all separate. My view is different from yours, different from anybody's – unless maybe someone were standing exactly where I am at exactly the same second and with exactly the same psychological and emotional output – which is virtually impossible. There are billions of separate people with billions of separate views.

When you profoundly see one view, you've seen them all.

How is that possible? You mean, everything is atoms, so everything is the same?

Everything is Pure Aware Emptiness, manifesting Itself via an infinite variety of ever-changing forms.

You're saying that none of this is real?

On the contrary, it's the only reality there is.

I'm sorry, I just don't understand.

Yes you do, deep inside the mask you're wearing. We're all hiders, and we take our hiding very seriously. But inside, at the core of you, you know. It's What You Are, and It manifests as the universe – which is What You Are in manifestation. It's Intelligence beyond comprehension, coming up with not only a universe, but with the mask behind which It hides from Itself – and even these words about Itself. And returning to what you said earlier, it's true that no one else in the world has your view because there is no one else in the world. You are First-Person-Singular, viewing yourself! Always, no matter where you look, all you see is yourself. Turn around, you are there, Pick up a rock, you are there. There is nowhere you are not. As you said, the view is reserved only for you. And anyone can say it.

But why are these views, these manifestations of What I Am, all different?

That's the dance. That's what we call "the universe." If they weren't different, there'd be no universe. Why do I manifest at all? I don't know. To realize myself, perhaps. To be. One explanation I've heard is that each individual view is that person's unique invitation to wake up, which of course would apply only to an assumed "person" who is asleep. I don't know. That's as good an explanation as any, I suppose. My answer is that it just is, in all its majesty and terror and beauty. It's God, being God.

Maybe someday I'll see what you mean. If I'm hiding, I don't realize it, and I'd sure like to be found.

If you want to be found, you will be. If you don't want to be found, you will be anyway.

REINCARNATION REVISITED

Do you believe in reincarnation?

I don't believe in anything. That way, I don't get confused.

Seriously, I got to thinking about reincarnation, and the expression "Wherever you go, there you are" came to mind. It relates with what you've said about Empty Awareness always being here, no matter what the scene.

Yes. A thousand years ago, right now, and two hundred years in the future, you'll be here – never arising, never passing away, never being anywhere or anywhen but right here.

But that's not to say that reincarnation can't happen, right?

From the point of view of Who You Really Are, the question of reincarnation makes no sense because you are not a separate one to be reincarnated. Nor is there a "past" or a "future" for it to happen in. In manifestation, if reincarnation happens, it's a dream-happening, and nothing more. It's of no importance. The only meaning it might hold is also within the dream – some might see it as proof that we are not the individuals we think we are. To Who You Really Are, this is frivolity. Only those who believe they are separate selves would be concerned about such things.

So why are there so many separate selves? How is it we have this mass hallucination going on?

It's the way it is. It's What Is, functioning. It's God doing a jig. How do I know?

Well, how do the awakened explain it?

Let me ask you, do you believe you're a separate self?

Yes.

Because?

Because I can't deny this sense of I Am. I know I'm not my name, my job, my personality, all that. I know that my body is just cells, and cells are molecules, atoms and particles. And science tells me that particles really aren't anything but mathematical probabilities. And I know that thoughts come and go and are always changing and aren't really anything either. So it comes down to this I Am, and although I can't say what it is, it's definitely here, and it's also unique – in other words, my I Am is mine and yours is yours.

Everyone experiences this sense of I Am. Everyone, if they look deeply enough, as you seem to have, can see that it is not something you can attribute to the body, or even the mind. It's not anything at all, and yet it's always here – I Am. Bodies and minds are different, but I Am is the same, right?

No. Well...

Is I Am a thing, an object?

No. It's an intuited sense, a knowing, but it's not a thing.

Then why say it's unique to you?

Because it's only here, inside me. And obviously you have a sense of I Am too, inside you. So they are separate I Ams.

I Am is impersonal, and somehow you've assumed it to be personal. In that assumption lies the distinction between absolute and relative, *nirvana* and *samsara*. In fact, however, there is no distinction because there is only one I Am, and it isn't *anything* at all. That which is nothing cannot be different or separate from "another" nothing – there cannot be two nothings! Everyone experiences I Am, and we're all taught as children that we're "over here" inhabiting this body, and we grow up learning that this I Am is a product of this particular body; from then on we apply it to "ourselves." It's an innocent mis-take, a misunderstanding, but it's fatal. The reality is, there are not separate I Ams inhabiting separate bodies. If anything, it's the other way around – apparently separate bodies inhabit I Am! This is why bodies are only *apparently* separate, why anything and everything is only apparently separate. The universe appears inside the embrace of I Am. Everything is I Am, appearing! There is only I Am, and that which arises and passes away, including all bodies and minds, is an *expression* of I Am.

So you're equating the sense of I Am with what you call Empty Awareness?

Yes.

For some reason, I didn't make the connection until just now.

It can be a startling connection to make.

It's not particularly what I wanted to hear about reincarnation, though. It's like I understand what you're saying about Empty Awareness, but I still clutch at the idea of reincarnation in an attempt to hold onto I Am.

When in fact you can't get *rid* of I Am! What you *are* is I Am. How could you hold onto what you are? Who is this "you" to hold onto anything?

But there's still the dream. How do I get out of the dream?

You don't! There's no need to get out. Isn't that marvelous? There's no waking up because there's no one asleep.
No-thing and everything, *nirvana* and *samsara*, reality and
the dream, are not two! There really is no dream. We simply
use the analogy of a dream to clarify the fact that reality is
not the belief that we are separate selves living in a world
of separate things. Believing this story, we are said to be
like "dream characters living in a dream." And when the
misunderstanding ends, it's not as if a new world emerges;
you aren't transported to a heavenly realm or a higher plane
of consciousness. Nothing really changes. There's no dream,
no awakening. Nor is there a dreamer, in case that last-ditch
attempt at selfhood happens to be standing by, ready to fill
the void.

So...the desk, the cup, the TV, the wall – all of it is...

Nirvana! There's no "something else." *Samsara* is *nirvana*,
right now, always.

But the sense of I Am....

Is the Absolute. I Am is not an entity. It is what appears,
what presents itself, what shows up. I Am and the scene are
the same. The scene is what I Am is, all that it can be said to
be. What you see is what you are, and there's no waking up
from what you are.

*Then what we call "awakening" is just the understanding that I
Am is no individual self.*

Basically, yes. And no world into which you are born and

against which you must struggle. However, it's more than an intellectual understanding. It's seen, and profoundly so.

By whom?

By no one. All I can say is that it's seen. Or perhaps: seen by Itself, and it isn't anything other than Itself.

So there's no fireworks? It's just a cup, a desk, a wall?

Ha! Yes. It's the same old same old, as they say. All very ordinary. Maybe even *more* ordinary, without the drama of selfhood. But don't confuse ordinary with boring – boring it isn't.

What is it, then?

Complete. Joyful. Sometimes hilarious. Amazing, considering that whatever shows up is what you are.

Including problems?

There are no problems. No mistakes. Nothing is "wrong." What I Am is what is, so how could there be a problem? A problem to whom?

And that would include a punch in the face?

That would include an H-bomb in your pants!

Sounds a little personal to me. I thought you said it was impersonal.

It's personal only until detonated.

Funny guy.

To clarify what I said earlier about I Am being impersonal, I have to add that it's both impersonal *and* personal, which I realize is no clarification at all, but there's no other way to put it. I Am, Empty Awareness, the Absolute, is entirely impersonal, and at the same time is ultra personal. It's beyond intimate. It's What You Are, being present with What You Are – and the term "being present with" does not for a moment convey the intended meaning. It's impersonal in that there is no "you" and no "other," and for that same reason it is also ultra personal. It's I Am, boiling within Itself, expressing Itself to Itself in continuous union.

Earlier you said that what is, is complete. What do you mean by "complete"?

When something is boring, it's because it's not enough. There's no contentment, no fulfillment. By the term "complete," I mean that each moment is the totality of itself, and there's no thought of having left something undone or of having something "next" to do. There's no "When I get this and this and this in order, then I can relax."

I noticed you didn't mention the word "bliss." Joyful and amazing, you said, but not blissful.

It can be blissful. It's not my experience that ordinary is blissful, but who am I to say? The potential difficulty with blissful, however, is that it can pose as "awakening" and be the target of endless grasping and attachment. It feels too good, and one can spend a lifetime trying to recreate the "high" obtained from a brief glimpse of the Absolute. Mystical experiences, like all other experiences, are not the Absolute, and not what is meant by the term "wisdom." For this reason you'll occasionally hear spiritual teachers say that those who haven't had blissful experiences are the lucky ones.

Bliss can be another form of suffering, then?

Exactly.

I don't think I have to worry too much about getting hooked on bliss. I do get these "Aha" moments, though, and it's like I'm always looking for the next one.

Yes, they too can be a trap. What comes and goes is not the Absolute. The Absolute is always here, never arising, never passing away. It's no one, and it's sensed as I Am. It's Empty Awareness, in which appear all the blissful and revelatory moments of a trillion lifetimes, not one of which could make the slightest difference to Empty Awareness.

Ah – see! You just said a trillion lifetimes! So there is reincarnation, after all!

Are we having an "Aha" moment?

Yes, I guess we are....

So there's hope, after all, that you'll go on existing forever and ever? Did I toss you a lifeline when you were falling?

Pretty stupid, huh?

No, not stupid. Never stupid. It's how this works, this play, this conversation. There's no separation here. It happens as one, and not even one. It appears to go out and back, and in that movement is Love. Thank you for this talk.

Yes, of course. And thank you.

148

FRIENDS

What about friends? Would you say that you have more friends or fewer friends since becoming interested in spiritual matters?

More friends. Why do you ask?

Well, a few see you as kind of an oddball, with some pretty strange ideas about how the world works.

How nice to hear!

So you don't think you scare people off?

I don't go around insulting people's beliefs. That would be rude, not to mention unkind. Nor do I try to insert my beliefs. Why would I do that? Everything is perfect just the way it is. If someone comes to me with a personal problem, I take them in exactly as they are. If it's a plumbing issue or a weird joke or a football score, that's what I am, just as it appears.

How do you define friendship, then? The usual definition is that it's two people, getting along.

That would be pretend friendship. Real friendship is when there is no one here but your friend. The truth is, a person is never intimate with another unless he or she is no longer a person.

How can you be intimate if you aren't even there?

As Empty Capacity for you, I take you in not partially, but completely. There is nothing here in the way, so I am what you bring, exactly as you bring it. What I Am is clear, awake, luminous Presence, filled with you. If that isn't intimacy, I don't know what is.

Is this your definition of love also?

Yes. Intimacy is love in action. It's dying, that you might live in me. You are my life. Without you, I have none.

So that you are my life also! And anyone can say the same. Can you imagine what the world would be like if everyone saw it this way? How did you come up with this wonderful theory?

I didn't come up with it. It's a gift from a friend, and from What I Am. And it's not a theory, it's fact. I *see* it, and many others see it, as well. Here, as Clear Essence, there is absolutely nothing in the way, nothing this side of you. You *replace* me. I'm out, you're in. All relationships are this way, face there to no-face here, whereas we are conditioned to believe we are "face-to-face" with someone. See for yourself. This isn't optional. It's how you're built, wide open for love. Everyone is a friend.

But say it's somebody you don't even know. Say I walk into the room, and you've never seen me before.

I immediately know you in two ways: First, I see that there is nothing this side of you, that you completely invade me. Therefore, you *are* me, all that is left of me. Second, I know that the core of both of us is the *same* Empty Awareness I see right here. Not your empty awareness there, and my empty awareness here, but the *same* Empty Awareness, God Himself. How do I know we are not two? There is nothing to be two of! Empty is just that: empty. Of nothing, there can be nothing to differ. What we are is not "we" at all. Only the word "I" will do, and I am The Alone, First-Person-Singular. So...not to see you as a friend would be absurd, no?

Would you agree, then, that seeing What You Are improves relationships?

Ultimately, there are no relationships, for who could be in relation to whom? But to answer your question: In the sense that there is no one here to relate to, no one confronting another – yes, relationships may improve. However, there are no expectations or predictions; there's no one in charge to dictate what will appear or how this body and mind will react. If a man attacks with a knife, it might run like hell or it might clobber him with a chair. Being open doesn't mean being a punching bag. In many situations, the kindest act might be to prevent someone from assaulting me, if for no other reason than to save him from the guilt and/or legal consequences he may incur. But even such kindly acts are not a matter of personal choice. What happens, happens.

Yes, but what about your personal motivation to harm another, to impose your will?

What I am has no will, no personal motivation. It is not possible to harm another.

Okay, but what about the person I call "you," the body and mind appearing before me – does it continue to play its role of self-interest?

Like I said, it will react according to its conditioning as that-which-appears. But the motivation to be unkind to others or to get something for itself – especially in the sense of scheming or acting at the expense of others – is gone.

Do you still have the same friends you used to?

Friends from my previous life? No. Friends here? Yes. Some, I think, tolerate me as "the old man," some probably consider me eccentric. They are – all of them – more than easy to love. And there are many new friends worldwide, all wonderfully open and clear. A great blessing, to be sure.

So you haven't wanted to retreat into silence like a monk in a cave?

No. Why do that? What's the difference between a cave and a crowded subway station? My "life" is whatever appears. Right now, you are my life. No matter what you bring, you invade me as a friend. It's a beautiful thing.

Even if I'm cussing you out?

Even then. You are a mirror image. If you're cussing me out, I'm cussing me out. Always, always, I get what I need, exactly when I need it. The world is a friendly place. It is by no means hostile.

It's good to have friends.

Yes, it is. And let me add that if I was selfish in a former life, I'm doubly selfish now. All of this is a glorious friendship with myself, for I am All That Is. I just didn't know it before.

DIVINE WORK

I read the Bhagavad-Gita *last week, and it talks about not being attached to outcomes. What do we do, then, just let any old thing happen?*

It simply means having no expectations as to results. Working for the sake of working, for instance, with no thought about your pay.

Well, I'm not working for nothing.

Actually, you are. You just don't realize it.

Are you kidding? If I've got a job and they don't pay me, I'll quit!

You can't quit what you are, and you don't get paid for that. What the *Bhagavad-Gita* is pointing out is that when you are attached to outcomes, you experience anxiety and worry – and when things don't work out the way you want – anger, disappointment, and guilt. Why go about your day stressed-out, when you can do whatever you do in peace?

So I can do the same thing I'm doing, but just not expect it to go the way it's supposed to?

You just do whatever – work, relax, write a letter – and when it's over, something else comes along. Isn't that the way it is anyway?

Yeah, I guess so.

So why add on all that business about "It's supposed to go this way or that"? It is what it is, and when you put expectations on it, you set up conditions for suffering.

But if I don't have expectations, I won't put much into it, you know? Like, if I don't expect to win, I won't, and if I don't expect to earn a certain amount, I won't work as well.

I don't find that to be true. Working for the sake of working, it more often goes smoothly, calmly, with fewer mistakes. And as for winning, how many times have we heard athletes talk of being "in the zone," how "automatic" and thought-free it is, or how it's all about this one point or one game, one game at a time? Attaching to outcomes could be the surefire way to lose.

I can see that this approach requires a different outlook altogether.

It's not that radical, although the principle behind it may appear to be. What we're talking about here is simply either doing what you do with the weight of the past and future on you, or remaining in the present and going with the flow.

So, what is the principle behind it?

That when there is work, you are the work. That there is no "you," there is only "working." That the work is a manifestation of the Absolute, and is therefore seen by many as sacred and to be performed as an act of consecration, in the spirit of dedication.

Dedication to whom?

154

To no one. To God, if you like.

But God is someone.

On the contrary, God is no one. God is All That Is. God is the worker, the work, and that which is worked. He is all of it, dedicating Himself to Himself.

Where do I come in?

You don't. Who you think you are is actually God, pretending to be "you."

Yeah, well, I see what you mean – this is pretty radical.

It's only radical when you're caught in the pretending. When the act ends – and it will end – you'll see that it's laughably ordinary, that it's your very nature, that it's What You Are!

In the meantime I think I'll try the working-for-the-sake-of-working part, see how that goes.

Of course. And while you're at it, don't expect to be any less stressed than you were. Don't expect to achieve anything by it. Don't expect an outcome for having no outcomes.

SOLIPSISM

The physicist Erwin Schroedinger once said, "Consciousness is a singular of which the plural is unknown." I assume this is what you meant when you said there is no such thing as multiple consciousnesses.

Yes. Consciousness is not a thing. It's nothing, so how can there be more than one of what isn't? How can there be even one of what isn't?

But it's definitely something. I'm conscious. You're conscious.

There is only Consciousness.

I still don't see it that way.

That's because you're *thinking* it that way. If you were to drop your assumptions, drop your preconceived ideas and actually *look*, you might see it for what it is. You've pointed back at what is looking and seen what you are, right?

Yes.

And is it boundless, empty, awake, filled with the scene, and right where you are?

Yes.

Have you ever seen it anywhere else?

No. But what about you? You're conscious.

How do you know that? Can you see that I have a separate consciousness?

No.

Then why take it for granted? This is about First-Person-Singular. Here – take this hand mirror and hold it up at arm's length next to my face, so that your face in the mirror and my face are about the same size, side by side. Now tell me, is there consciousness in the mirror face?

No, it's over here where I am.

So why afford consciousness to the other face, my face? They are both appearances, both reflections.

Now put the mirror down and stand over here next to me, so that we're both looking in the same direction, with essentially the same scene presented to us. Stretch out an arm to the side, and I'll do the same to the other side. Now – notice that you are holding one single Eye, one Consciousness, and for a flesh body you have two arms, two trunks, and four legs – all inside your one Conscious Eye. This Awake Emptiness is what you are, and it *can't* be plural. It is one Seeing by all.

All the same, this way of looking seems dangerously self-centered, don't you think?

Do you find me or anyone else – anything whatsoever – less worthwhile, less loveable, seeing that you alone are Consciousness?

No. In fact, it seems more the opposite. I get a feeling of wanting to care for others.

Because they are you? Are *inside* of you?

Yes.

This is how it is, and don't ask me why. It's just love loving itself. But since you mentioned the possibility of it being dangerously self-centered, you might want to look again. This is another of those instances when, although what you are can immediately be seen, it could take hours of mental gymnastics to explain that which is essentially unexplainable, so it's worth looking.

If you cut the end off a paper bag and place one end against the bathroom mirror and your face in the other, you'll notice that all the matter is at the far end and all the Consciousness is at the near end. Once you see this, it's obvious that it's always this way, without the device, no matter where you look. As Zen master Po-Shan said, "Only when you find no things in Consciousness, and no consciousness in things, are you empty and spiritual, formless and marvelous."

It's essential, however, that you identify with what is seen at the near end – Awake No-thing, what we've referred to as First-Person-Singular, which is not an object. Believing there is matter at this end, or consciousness at that end – whether it is a mirror face or someone else's face at that end – is contrary to what you see, and is the basis of the "sin" of dualism. When you see yourself as an object, you see others as objects. When you see you are unmitigated Subjectivity, you also see others as Subjectivity – as what you are. Subjectivity is not personal. God is I, I am not God. There is all the difference in the world in that statement.

So what we are talking about here is not the solipsism of the third-person, which can truly be a hellish situation, both for that so-called "individual" and others around him. This would be like saying, "I alone exist as this separate self, and all of you are my objects to do with as I please." Rather, what we are talking about is the solipsism of God, of First-Person-Singular, Present Tense. It is not the heresy of two existences, "mine" and God's, but the truth of God alone. It is not the heresy of multiple consciousnesses, but the truth of All Is Consciousness. Not the heresy of exclusion, but the truth of inclusion. It is saying, "I am not, God alone is," because all see from the Eye of God. The Aware No-thing I see Here is the *same* Aware No-thing that all see from, and seeing this, how could you exclude others, see others as objects, use others? As First-Person-Singular, the danger of egoism does not arise.

I hear what you are saying, and identifying with what is seen is obviously the key, but how do I keep that up, or what can I do to remind myself that I'm not this ego?

Well, again, this isn't up to ego. Why impose additional bondage, not to mention baggage? God does what He wants, when He wants, which is what we call "reality." Furthermore, it's what you are, so why attribute what you do to a separate self?

Yes. That's a relief, isn't it?

It's loving yourself. How do you love yourself? The same way you love others, from the same Empty Space. You really can't do it any other way, so why pretend otherwise?

Seeing this Emptiness is really seeing everyone else, isn't it? I mean, it's what everyone is, and what everyone is looking out of. Wow! This is huge! It's the true meaning of empathy, isn't it? Actually being others, or rather, seeing from the same essence everyone else does!

Yes. It's the true meaning of compassion. It's what Buddhists call *bodhichitta*. It's love loving itself. It includes all that appears within its embrace, which of course is itself. Incidentally, Erwin Schroedinger also said, "Our perceiving self is nowhere to be found within the world-picture because it itself is the world-picture."

WILL

I read an article awhile back in one of those science magazines about tests that were performed to determine how long it took a person to act after deciding to do something – if I remember correctly, it involved moving a hand – and in tracking the electrical signals in the nervous system, the surprising result was that the neuronal impulses were discovered to fire a fraction of a second before the subject decided to move his hand!

Yes, I read that also. I can't remember the details, but if it's true – that is, if it's been repeated in other subjects, and so on – I'd say it lends credence to the idea that there is no personal motivation. And where there's no personal motivation, there's no person to have it.

The implications are staggering, when you think about it. It means that everything I ever decided to do or not do was already put into motion before I decided it!

Yes, so who decided it?

That's what I want to know! And this is science saying this, not some new age doctor of reflexology or Hindu holy man in a diaper.

That's *dhoti.*

Okay, dhoti.

I don't know about new age doctors, but Hindu holy men have been saying it for ages, that the ego cannot act, that only the Self is and does everything.

So who is the Self?

The Self isn't a who or a what or anything at all, yet the Self is the foundation, the fountain, of everything in the universe. It's You, without the baggage of believing you're a separate body and mind. Someone once said that awakening is a matter of boarding a train and leaving your luggage behind, which is a good metaphor, although leaving the luggage is not something you can purposely do, nor is it necessary. It's simply a matter of seeing through a false identity. What remains is what you are. If the false identity travels with you, no big deal – you no longer have to believe it.

I'm still stuck on this volition thing. It's really hard to accept that I'm not deciding or choosing to do things, minute by minute. Choice, or free will, is the cornerstone of our society. I can't believe I'm an automaton, run by someone called a Self!

Ha! No, no – the Self is not an entity, not some old man inhabiting a chunk of space just the other side of the Milky Way. In regards to volition, when you see what you are, there's no question about whether or not you do or don't do anything. Only when you think you're separate do these questions arise.

I still don't understand how my hand moves if I don't consciously do it.

How does your blood circulate? How do you sweat or digest your food or fall asleep? And is it you who moves your hand, or did the 15 billion cells of your body get together and decide to move a section of their own?

So why do I even decide to move my hand – or pretend to

decide – after the neuronal impulses fire? Why aren't I just ignorant of the situation altogether?

Apparently a thought accompanies the impulse.

But I'm the thought! I'm the one having the thought.

It only seems that way. Thoughts simply appear like anything else, and they appear as part of what they are thoughts about; they are attached to things or events of the apparent world. Ask anyone who meditates if thoughts can be controlled, or if thoughts can be stopped, even for a minute. It's impossible. Thoughts come out of nowhere and disappear into nowhere, like everything else.

Then where am I?

You are awareness of thoughts, awareness of movement, awareness of everything that appears in awareness, so you are nowhere and everywhere.

Well what about this body? Is it just walking and talking on its own? Please don't say yes.

It's not doing anything on its own. It may seem to be, but so do your organs or cells or atoms if examined apart from their interconnections. Obviously the body couldn't do without cells or organs, but neither could it do without the biosphere or Earth or the sun, not for a second. The body is simply part – and not even a part – of a continuous interconnected infinity called a "universe," which is awareness manifesting. You are that. Your only body is the Whole Body.

So I'm not doing anything.

No. It's been said that, as who you think you are, you're

being done. "Not my will, Lord, but Thine."

And I'm not thinking?

You're being thought.

This is too weird to be frightening, but it's frightening just the same. But there's also a tiny glimmer of relief, because if it's true, it means I don't have to feel ashamed of the things I've done in the past, or worried about what I might do in the future.

Yes, there are no mistakes. No one can do it wrong. Guilt, pride, hatred, arrogance – all fall away when you give up the reins. As who you think you are – a separate self – you have no control over the events of the world, no control over the body, no control over thoughts, precisely because there is nothing separate. What you really are is the Whole Deal. If you don't agree with this or if you hang me as a heretic, even that is the All being the All. As they say, it's all good.

But what about my personality, my uniqueness – my finger-prints, even? I'm not some blob of protoplasm oozing through life.

No, you are far less and far more. You are Aware No-thing and the ever-changing Everything that appears in it. What you take to be your self – your body and mind – is one such appearance. You could see it as you might a flower, including all that it took to produce such a marvelous specimen. Without it, there would be no universe, for everything that appears is connected to everything else. The universe is a perfectly orchestrated dance in which your body-mind is a choreographed step. A *unique* step.

Don't you think this is dangerous information? If I see I have no responsibilities because I'm not the doer of anything, I could run amok and not care about who I hurt.

How would that be possible if you are not the doer? And anyway, in my experience, just the opposite is true. When you realize you're not the doer, you realize what you really are, and what that is is beyond beautiful, beyond astonishing, beyond precious. Gratitude pours out of it. Love.

And others? I take it they aren't doing anything either, so is that the end of blame?

Exactly! Actually, there are no others.

This is pretty mind-boggling. I want to listen to what you're saying because there's a part of me that resonates with it, but the greater part resists. It has to do with my thinking, my actions, my personality, the way I go about my daily life that I know is similar to others but is also unique. I can't just wave that off and say it doesn't happen, that it's not me doing something my way.

It does happen. There's just no individual "you" behind it. The mind is a bundle of thoughts, the body is flesh, and both are subject to a complicated web of conditioning, so that what is done is done as a result of that. This is what appearance is; it's how it unfolds. Let's say you profoundly realize you are not a separate self. Even so, what the personality does, how it responds, may not change. Everything may go on as usual. The only difference is that you no longer identify with that separate self.

I know I keep saying this, but the sense of "being," of "I," is so strong that I can't accept that no one is here and doing these things. If it's not me, there has to be some kind of replacement, you know?

Yes. The comfortable replacement is God. It's, shall we say, a step in the right direction: out with "you," in with God. Another way of saying it is that the sense of "being" you feel is actually nothing, which, being awake, is not simply nothing but a very special nothing, so we refer to it as No-thing; and also, because it is not simply nothing but is absolute nothing, it is Everything. So – you are No-thing/Everything. Which, let me add, doesn't begin to describe what This is. Maybe the most appropriate replacement is silence, which is truer, and which won't further strain our sensibilities, not to mention our tongues. Amen?

Yes. Amen. For now.

RESPONSIBILITY

Returning to the subject of personal volition, you said that I'm not the doer of my acts, which is the same as saying I'm not responsible for anything I do. Is that correct?

It depends on where you place your identity. As who you think you are, as a body and mind, you are in no way responsible. That body-mind is simply one appearance in an infinity of interconnected appearances, all moving as one. Thus, how it acts depends on how an infinity of other appearances act.

So it's the butterfly effect taken to the limit.

Yes. There's no end to it. Causes extend to infinity, past and future alike, which, by the way, is the same as saying that there are no causes, that nothing has ever happened or will happen. When science says there is no center to the universe, it also means that the center is everywhere.

So you're saying that I don't do anything, that this body only acts according to its conditioning and to the circumstances at hand?

It *reacts*. It's part hardware, part software, and responds according to genetic and environmental conditioning. Locally, these influences may be obvious, but at a distance the weave is endlessly complicated. This is why everything is precious. I get a card in the mail from a friend, and I know that it took the whole universe to produce this card, and here it is. The abbreviated version is: Big Bang, galaxy, solar system, Earth, biosphere, life, soil, water, tree, paper – and at each amazing juncture there are an infinite number of contributing factors, right down to the mail carrier and the cells, molecules, atoms and particles of the hand that places it in the box. And at no point along this endless chain of activity is there a personal actor.

But how could our society or any society exist without a sense of responsibility? There would be chaos, anarchy.

There wouldn't have to be. Do you hold weeds responsible for growing on your lawn? No. You simply dig them up. We're a nation of blamers. A natural disaster occurs, and for a year we hear about who didn't do what to prevent such and such. It's the land of the lawsuit, and the fear is, without blame, everything will fall apart. But suppose there were only solutions, offered in a framework of love, or even awe. Would there be chaos? It's curious also that most people think that the cure for blame is for one to take personal responsibility, but actually the cure for blame is for one to realize the absence of personal responsibility altogether. Blaming oneself is no different than blaming another. It merely perpetuates the game of separate self.

It's true, however, that the way things are is the way they should be. The fact that humanity confuses Presence with personal selfhood, and from that assigns to each the onus of responsibility for their thoughts and acts, is the way things are right now, and is therefore the natural order of appearance – until it changes. It's actually perfect the way it is, because it is this way. Which is the only sane way to see it, no?

I guess. But not everyone agrees, obviously.

No. And that too is the way it is. A few see through the game, see that they *are* the game and all of the players in it, quarks to galaxies. It is these few who see that they are *totally* responsible, that the responsibility lies with This and no one else because there is no one else. Claiming authorship, they claim responsibility for all that is. And in so doing, discover it to be good.

What I really am does it all? You're saying that I'm the only doer, and therefore I'm the only one responsible?

I'm saying that you're the doer, all of the doing, and all of what's done. Ask me some other time, and I'll say there's no doer and nothing is done. Take your pick.

So who's to blame?

Exactly.

WHAT YOU SEE IS WHAT YOU GET

When you say that all of the things of this world are really only Presence, do you mean that everything is illusory, that none of this is really here?

No, I don't mean that. What you see is what you get. It's illusory as what you think it is, but it's as really here as "really here" can be. It's What You Are, appearing. Incidentally, it's beautiful, don't you think?

Well... not from where I'm standing.

Then you're missing a great show. And in case you're wondering, I'm seeing the same thing you are.

How can you say it's beautiful?

It's not so much *what* it is, it's *that* it is, that's beautiful. It's Here. It's appearing. It's What I Am, appearing to Itself! It's amazing!

It's a desk, a lamp, a metal stool and a cement wall. What's so amazing about that?

It could be nothing. Absolutely zilch. Just a blank, unaware that it's blank. But incredibly, the impossible is happening—it's no-thing appearing as something, wide awake to Itself!

You're really out of your tree, you know that?

Oh yes. Thanks to This! To be in one's tree is to be insane.

Let's get back to what you call Presence. If the things of this world are only appearances of Presence, then how could they be real?

As what you think they are – as self-existing in the world – they aren't real. That goes for you also. There's no "you" here and "things" over there. And I can say this until the cows come home, and it won't make any difference. You've seen What You Are, you've looked within, and yet you continue to believe the story you've been handed down from others. This is the power of conditioning.

Yes, that's true, I can't stop what I believe, despite what you've shown us. I guess it's because what I see is just too radical, too opposite of the way I learned to think of myself in the world.

Even though you can plainly see that it's not true, that, in fact, the world is in you!

Yes.

This is the difference between seeing and thinking. What you see is what you get; what you *think* is an illusion. It's akin to the Buddhist formula 1.) First there are mountains and rivers; 2.) then there are no mountains and rivers; 3.) then once again there are mountains and rivers. First, you believe you are a separate self in a world of separate things; then, looking within, you see you are pure, empty Subjectivity; and finally, seeing correctly, you see you are filled with the scene, that subject and object are one, all right Here. Thus, mountains and rivers are once again mountains and rivers, but as What You Are. What you thought you were is replaced by the scene, is now "mountains and rivers," your very appearance and the only reality you have. This is not something you can think your way to, not something you can accept on faith. It must be *seen* to be believed, and even then, seeing does not always lead to believing.

The odd thing is that I keep coming back wanting more in the way of explanation from you. It's like I'm caught, knowing inside that what I've seen is true, but not trusting it and wanting to disprove it, to trip you up so I can say, Aha! – you were wrong and I was right!

Have the courage to be what you see.

Easier said than done.

Actually, it's not difficult at all. In fact, you're doing it anyway, whether or not you acknowledge it. You can't do otherwise, you can't do it wrong, you can't be anything but What You Really Are – you just think you can. We're all pretenders, but we're only pretending. Pretending is actually the hard part. All day long we're acting out the role that others have assigned to us, pretending we're what others say we are from where they are.

Still, it takes courage to be what we see, doesn't it?

It's the meaning of warriorship, of knighthood, of The Quest. *You* are the Holy Grail. The irony is that you can't find what you're searching for because it's too close, because you already are it. So yes, it takes courage, but it's also the easiest thing in the world.

WHAT IS, IS

One of the things that helped to break down my view of the world as consisting of solid, self-existing objects was an elementary knowledge of small-particle physics, how everything that seems solid is actually made up of smaller and smaller parts – molecules, atoms, particles, quarks and, finally, mostly empty space. Ultimately, matter is energy.

Yes, that can help. However, at the moment, this is a concept. You don't go around seeing particles, sticking your hand through walls, and so on.

No, but I know how things really are, so....

In fact, things are how they are presented, exactly as they are presented. There is no such thing as fixed size.

But with an electron microscope, I can prove that things aren't as they are presented. That desk there would reveal itself to be made of atoms, for instance.

Looking through an electron microscope, you are Awareness at the level of atoms. You are an atom looking at your counterpart, which is the same as looking at yourself. You are, as they say, a "nuclear physicist." Likewise, in an observatory, you are a galaxy looking at a galaxy, a star at a star, a planet at a planet. Always you are looking at yourself, exactly as you are presented to yourself.

I don't understand how you can say there is no fixed size. Right in this room there are dozens of things of different size. That cup, for instance, is smaller than the lamp, the lamp is smaller than the desk, etcetera.

It depends on how you see them. I say there is no fixed size because ultimately there is nothing separate. Nor is there distance. Distant from what? The ideas of fixed size and distance are linked to the idea of a separate self. Conversely, taking what is presented, exactly as it is presented, is What You Are as What Is. In the world of appearance, size and distance are learned; they require thought, based on memory. Television is an example. Looking at the show currently on, you don't see everything two-dimensionally on the screen, but assume a three-dimensional "TV-world" in which the action occurs. Actually, of course, it's happening two-dimensionally on the screen.

The same is true of what we call "reality." You assign a fixed size to a cup. It maybe appears as a very tiny cup, and you say it is at a *distance* of 50 feet from you, when actually it is presented right here *as a very tiny cup*. Bring the cup all the way up to you, and you say it is "close," but actually it's a cup so huge it blocks out the horizon. The cup is exactly as you see it; any previous cup is a memory. Nor is the cup a vast assemblage of atoms – it's a cup! Or more precisely, it's what we *call* a cup.

The key here is to look back at what you're looking out of and take for true exactly what you see. In place of a head, for instance, you have a cup! In every instance, in place of a head, you have every appearance imaginable, *exactly as it appears*. This is good news for three reasons: 1.) You don't have a self to get in the way; 2.) you don't have to worry about what happens because you can't do anything about what appears or doesn't appear; and 3.) you don't have a face to project – the other guy has it!

Poor guy.

That poor guy happens to be me, right now, and I was going to ask you about that haircut. Who did it, a tree surgeon?

SUFFERING

I'd like to ask you about suffering and how you respond to it. Yours, and anyone else's.

There is no suffering. Suffering in only a story of suffering. It isn't real.

What about the suffering that the Buddha talked about? Was he wrong?

No. He addressed the *story* of suffering, the *appearance* of suffering, due to ignorance of What One Really Is.

But what about the people starving in refugee camps in Africa? Or India—you've been to India—what about the people living and dying on the streets? Or say a car flips over in front of you and catches fire and the driver is trapped. That's not suffering? What do you say to him, it's not real?

No, of course not. I do all I can, as quickly as I can. I don't think about it, I act. Nor do I say, "That's me in that car, I'd better get myself out!" There's no thought. You just respond, because it's all you. Where there are no stories of life and death, everything happens naturally, spontaneously, exactly as it should.

Suppose I tell you I'm having a relationship problem with a friend, and it's driving me nuts?

If you come to me and ask for help, I can't refuse, because you're What I Am. If you don't ask for help, I may nod in acknowledgement, but it's not my business to interfere or to tell you you're wrong, because from my point of view, nothing is ever wrong, and your story is your story until you see otherwise. Nor will I believe it.

Well I believe it!

That's your problem.

But you're a good Buddhist, you see I'm suffering, so don't you at least try to do something?

I'm not a good Buddhist, and I may do nothing about your perceived suffering. How do I know you need something done? Then again, I may respond if I perceive you are harming or about to harm yourself or others. This is elementary human behavior, whether or not you're open to it, but especially easy if you're open – that is, open all the way.

Meaning?

Meaning that you see What You Are, and that suffering is only a story told by others who don't yet see. Or rather, *apparent* others who don't see. Speaking of Buddhism, are you familiar with the Heart Sutra?

Yes, I've read it several times.

Then you're familiar with the line containing the phrase "no suffering, no end of suffering"?

Yes.

That would be a commentary on the *story* of suffering, don't you think?

Yes, I suppose.

There really isn't any other kind.

But what about bodily pain?

It's just pain. Pain is a sensation, nothing more. And incidentally, it's less severe without the story of suffering attached to it. It comes, it goes. But call it suffering, it's not only pain, it's a pain in the ass!

So having no agenda is the key.

Well, yes, but having no agenda is a result of profoundly seeing What You Are. You can't just go into a situation and say you won't have an agenda. With that, you've not only got the cart in front of the horse, you've got no horse.

Would you say that your response to suffering applies to other areas as well, like the environment, endangered species, abuse of animals, etcetera?

Yes, of course, it's all What I Am, and without the narrative, the response is immediate. I see trash, I pick it up. I find a wounded bird, I try to help. I shoo a spider out of harm's way. It's all so easy because there's so much gratitude in it.

But you weren't always this way.

Oh good heavens, no! It was all about me, number one. There were occasional exceptions, of course, but most of the time I was an extremely constricted and selfish character.

How did that feel?

Terrible. It was hell.

So would you say you were suffering?

Yes, I was deeply caught in the story of a separate "me." It's the beginning and end of what suffering is – the story of a separate "me." It's perhaps the *only* story.

The story of number one is the foundation to all other stories?

Yes. Some call it the original sin. Fortunately, it's only a story, told by no one. And realizing this, you realize there is nothing that can cause suffering because there is nothing other than What You Are. Who is there to suffer what?

Story equals hell. No story equals heaven.

Well put.

GOD WEARS MANY DISGUISES

You say that everything is an appearance of What I Am. I don't understand how that can be. Even if I look within and see I am No-thing, I still don't see how the scene is an appearance *of that.*

Well, the scene appears in No-thing. No-thing does not appear in the scene. Only objects, only things change, while this No-thing that you are does not – it's always the same. There's nothing Here that *could* change. Another way of saying it is that objects depend on Awareness, but Awareness does not depend on objects. Nothing could appear without Awareness to be aware of it. And you could make a case for the fact that you can never see an object as it really is. You can't see the back of it or the inside of it; you can't see what it really is all at once. You can only see *appearances* of it.

Those aren't very convincing arguments. At least not to me.

Okay. Then how about the Buddhist doctrine of impermanence? Things don't last. Everything appears and disappears. A sub-atomic particle comes and goes in a millisecond, a galaxy in billions of years. Nothing lasts forever. Even the universe will eventually disappear. What You Are, however, is timeless, beyond time, prior to time. There is no-thing Here to come or go!

Still....

In that case, let's try something that brings home the meaning of "appearance" like no other. It's a thought experiment about an observer-scientist who is determined to find out what you are made of, what you really are.

He's equipped, as it were, with a special homing device which will lead him directly to you. He begins at the outer edge of the universe, where he sees nothing but empty space. Following the homing device, and traveling at great speed, eventually he spots a tiny point of light in the distance. Approaching it, the light grows brighter and takes on a spiral shape. "Well," he figures, "this must be what you are: a galaxy." But when he comes all the way up to you, he loses you, and finds in place of a galaxy a scattering of billions of stars. From a distance, you appeared to be a galaxy; he was certain he had found you, and now he sees differently.

But wait! The homing device is pointing toward one of the stars in the galaxy. "So you're a star!" he announces, and heads toward you, only to find when he arrives that you are not a star at all. At a distance, you appeared to be a star, but now the homing device is pointing to a planet, one of the many that are circling the star.

"Now I've got you!" he decides, but again, when he goes all the way up to you, he loses you as a planet and discovers you are a continent, then a city on the continent, then a house in the city, then a human being in the house. "Maybe this is you," he thinks, now more than suspicious that you may not be what you appear to be. And sure enough, when he goes all the way up to you, he loses you as a human being and finds instead a vast assemblage of individual cells.

Still following the homing device, he finds you are one cell, then loses you as a cell and discovers you are molecules, then one molecule, then atoms, then one atom, then particles - and finally, close now, he discovers you are once again mostly empty space. On his journey toward you, every one of your appearances turned out to be just that – an appearance.

But he isn't all the way to you, yet. He's very close, but in order to find out what you truly are, he must turn around and look *out* with you, assume your point of view – and when he does, he is startled, for he sees that you are capacity for all of your appearances: pure, awake, empty capacity, filled with all the things you appear as! He concludes that you are No-thing, manifesting as Everything.

So, does that answer your question?

Yes, that works. What I appear as is determined by the observer's distance from me.

Exactly. We grow up believing we are human beings because that's what others have told us we are, because, for them, *from where they are*, that's what we appear as!

So everything I'm looking at right now is actually Me in disguise, Me as I'm appearing.

Bravo!

Because anything I go all the way up to, I lose!

Yes. And...?

And find empty space, no-thing, which is what I am!

Yes, and of course, wherever you are, there you are. There Awareness is. And always, always, wherever you are is *Here*.

This does work. It throws me back on myself. It's a thought-experiment, but it's based on science.

"Thou knowest not what thou hast wrought," I say to science.

And yet, I think the story wouldn't have been clear to me had I not actually looked within and seen No-thing – this Emptiness, as Buddhists call it – or what you call Awake Capacity.

Yes. Without *seeing* what you are, it's just another story.

So let me ask you, what am I for you?

You are an appearance of What I Am. How do I know that? There aren't two of you, an image here and a real you there, because when I go all the way up to you, I lose you. There remains only What I Am – aware, unchanging, empty – and when I turn and look out as you, all I see are appearances of every shape and color and texture imaginable, all the "things," or "you's," of this world, every one of which I could go up to and lose and find only Me, That Which I Really Am.

And anyone can say this?

Of course. There's no separation. It's all Awareness. We may appear to be different, but as we've just proven, what we appear to be is What I Am – No-thing appearing as anything and everything!

This is heavy stuff!

Actually, it's not. It's the natural way of seeing. Acting the part of a separate self is the heavy stuff – "heavy" as in "lost," or maybe just plain "nuts." Experiencing What You Are can at times be exhilarating, such as when you're walking somewhere and you realize you're walking through *yourself*. But really, it's the natural order of it. "Be yourself," they say. Well, okay, I think I am. I'm sitting in a world of myself talking to myself! How much more Me can I be?

Hee hee! That's hilarious!

You are hilarious! And by the way, why are you wearing that disguise, the one that looks like you but is What I Am?

Because what I appear as is What You Are, and what you appear as is What I Am, and they are One?

Yes.

Could we say that God wears many disguises?

We could, and others already have.

RE-APPEARANCE

On the subject of appearances again, does the scene appearing in front of me actually come from What I Am? I understand that the scene is an appearance of What I Am, but does that mean that this No-thing produces all that? Am I projecting it?

No. What You Are is No-thing and Everything, and one does not produce the other. However, it is not true to say that they arise together because No-thing never arises nor passes away, while Everything is continually arising and passing away. All I can say is that You are *both* the Center and the Circumference, but not as two. The "mistake" occurs when attending to one and not the other. To ignore No-thing and focus only on things "out there" – even to the point of assuming that what you are is a thing, an individual living in a world of individual things – surely that is an absurdity. It is the definition of ignorance.

And likewise, to ignore appearances and focus only on Aware No-thing, is absurd. Some have made the point that it is necessary to focus on No-thing because we are so deeply conditioned to focus elsewhere, and this has its value. We have suggested in our conversations that this Void is primary, prior to all else. But the truth is that neither No-thing nor Everything is fundamental to the other, that neither produces nor is prior to the other, *because they are not two. Nirvana* is *samsara*, and vice versa. There is void, and there is form, and the reality of both is Void/Form.

Then where does all this come from? Where does Awake No-thing come from?

Who knows? Who is there separate to know? If it blows your mind, it's blowing God's mind. God pulls himself up out of absolutely nothing by his own bootstraps, and has no idea how he does it.

I've been going over that observer-scientist thought-experiment you told me, and even though I get the point, the only thing that occasionally trips me up is the idea that there are two observers – the scientist heading toward me, and me. And also the fact that the observer-scientist has to turn around and look out with me in order to see what I am in manifestation.

Well, then we can eliminate the observer-scientist, and bring out the heavenly mirrors. Say you stand in front of a mirror, and from a distance of six feet, you see your appearance as a human being. Now we hang a giant mirror in the sky above the city, and you see yourself not as a human being but as a city. Hang a mirror on the moon, and you see you're a planet. Hang a really colossal mirror out in space, you're a star. And so on.

Yes, of course. That works as well as the observer-scientist, if not better. I repeatedly lose what I appear to be as the mirror recedes, just as the scientist loses what I appear to be as he approaches. Both stories get the point across, but I like the idea of only one observer.

Because the only observer is No-thing, Subject, First-Person. And that's first-person-*Singular.*

Yes.

It is also First-Person-Singular, *present tense.*

The Alone, only Here, only Now.

And not even that.

Well... how much closer can one get?

True. The great majority of stories lead away from This Which You Are. A very few lead toward You, and in that sense, your words are well spoken. Words that lead to the door and pry it open ever-so-slightly are precious gems, not to be dismissed. At the same time, they are words – concepts – and *must* be dismissed, for they will never suffice. Only *Seeing* will do, for Seeing is Being. Only God sees, and He sees only Himself.

IT'S CALLED FREEDOM

People talk a lot about freedom, but the more I think about it, the more I don't know what it is.

Yes, freedom is like fulfillment – no one seems to know what it is because it's always just out of reach. About the best you can do is aspire to it. The irony is, no one has ever been bound.

Because what I am is not a separate self?

Yes. What you are is everything, aware of what you are.

A question I sometimes ask is, What am I trying to get free from?

Well, that would be your identity as a separate self, the root of the sense of bondage, projected out into the world as whatever you think is binding you: job, family, political or social injustice, imprisonment, and so on. It's part of the game, and so we have a "life" in the pursuit of money, power, fame, even spiritual awakening – anything that might deliver the elusive state of freedom.

As much as I know better, I can't get past the idea that it would be so much easier to drop the belief that I'm a separate self if I were out of prison. I could go to retreats, hang out with other spiritual seekers, live in the mountains or some other quiet place, meet a guru – all that I can't do here. Do you ever feel that way?

No. There are no ideas of being somewhere other than where I am, nor of preferring what you call "anywhere else" to be here in me. If such a thought arrives, it quickly leaves. How could I feel bound by what I am?

Sometimes I really feel trapped, almost to the point of panic. The idea that there's no way out scares the hell out of me.

Well, in that case, you might have found the key to the problem. Scaring the hell out of you could leave you with heaven! There's maybe something to be said for being pushed into a corner. If you were out there in the world, you'd probably go from one situation to another, on and on spinning the same old story about finding freedom somewhere else or through someone other than you. Here, there's nowhere to go, and the world keeps slapping you in the face until you're on your knees in the corner, and finally a voice tells you to try the one direction you haven't yet tried: within. And incidentally, that world slapping you in the face happens to be yourself.

The thing is, I know there's no way out, that this is as good as it gets – and I'm talking about life, not prison – but I can't seem to accept it, at least not yet.

Yes, of course. But there's a flip side to that, which is that you were never *in*. Look, and *see* what you are, and forget accepting or not accepting. It's Presence. *You* are Presence, and the whole fabulous show is going on inside of You. How could you be in anything, if everything is You? You are First-Person-Singular, The Alone. How much freer could you be? To The Alone, questions of freedom and bondage do not arise.

Seeing I'm The Alone doesn't make me feel any freer. In fact, that scares the hell out of me too!

189

So we're getting to the nitty-gritty here. Who you think you are is losing its grip and afraid of falling into the abyss of Who You Really Are?

Yes, that's probably what's happening.

Well, take heart. There's no abyss. All I can suggest is that you stay with it, let the fear play itself out, if you can. There's absolutely nothing you can do about it anyway.

So what will happen to me?

Nothing. You'll still be around. You simply won't believe you're separate anymore. And you'll notice that you're in a very beautiful place that isn't really a place. It's called Freedom, and it's What You Are.

THE HAMSTER WHEEL

What did you do to wake up?

I didn't wake up. I was never asleep.

But surely there was a time when you believed you were a separate self.

That appeared. So what?

Then what did you do? How did you get past that?

My guess is that there are two things you want from this conversation: 1.) A method you or others can follow; and 2.) legitimacy of your separate self. There has to be a plan, or all is lost, no? It's called "Let's make a deal with Reality – if I do this and this, maybe I'll get to wake up and keep my separate self." Knowing what I went through, at least then you've got something to measure yourself by, or perhaps a new path you can try. And on and on you go, stuck on the hamster wheel of life.

A little testy today, aren't we?

Ha! Okay, okay... There were LSD sessions in the '60s, then a long bout with fear and nihilism and alcoholism, then in prison nine or ten years of daily meditation and Dharma training, then the vision to end all visions – the Beatific Vision – thanks to a simple look, suggested by a wise Englishman. The rest is history-less.

So you wouldn't recommend the same?

If I were to recommend something, it would be to see exactly what arises and what it arises *in*. Look, and look back. Have a look at yourself, and see what you are. It's so ridiculously obvious, so hilariously close, people miss it.

Do you regret your criminal past?

Of course. And I also know that whatever appears is what is supposed to appear, exactly as it appears. I don't know why. To question it is pointless. The past, from the Big Bang right up to this very moment, is a narrative that can only be told here and now, and even here and now are already gone. Truth is uncompromising. You don't get to shed the bad and keep the good, because it's *all* a narrative of and by That Which You Are. This may sound cold and heartless, but the opposite is true. Truth is love in its purest form. It's unconditional. I don't know why, it just is.

Then you deny any responsibility for the harm you've caused?

On the contrary, I'm responsible for it all. As the author of all that appears, how could I not be responsible for it? It all happens Here. Nothing has ever happened elsewhere. There *is* no elsewhere. This – all of it – is it!

THE GRAND SCHEME OF THINGS

*Every guy at the meeting this week said he had become interest-
ed in spiritual matters because of a fundamental dissatisfaction
with life, but no one could say what that dissatisfaction was.
One guy described it as the "cosmic itch he couldn't scratch." Is
that how it was for you?*

Yes and no. There was a vague sense of unease since child-
hood that seemed to worsen with age, but there was also
later in life a total collapse, a bottoming out.

A "dark night of the soul"?

Yes, I suppose you could call it that. A peculiar form of it.

Depression?

A profound sense of emptiness, interpreted as worthlessness,
which in turn gave rise to anger and destructive behavior.

And now?

Gone.

How do you explain that?

The emptiness that for so long I had considered a fault
became that it had always been: divine.

What you thought was your emptiness became the Emptiness?

Yes. The one and only.

But why call it divine?

What else could "divine" possibly mean? The Emptiness we're talking about is at the core of everything *is*, in fact, everything. It is awake. It is What I Am. It is what we all are, and since everything appears within its embrace, it is nothing less than the creator of the universe. How much more divine could it be?

I guess I was associating the word "divine" with God.

Emptiness, God, Buddha-mind, Brahma, The Beloved – call it what you will, it's the core of everything. Everything that appears is an appearance of it.

How could anyone see that as a fault?

It's puzzling, isn't it? I learned as a child that I was an individual, a solid and separate self. And as I grew older I began to feel this emptiness at my core as a gaping hole, one that I tried to fill with everything under the sun, failing all the while and growing more and more frustrated. It started out as an innocent mistake innocently learned, and progressed, in my case, into a calamity of major proportions.

And then – poof! – it was gone?

No, not poof! With so many years of conditioning, the sense of worthlessness dissipated slowly, although the destructive behavior ended immediately. All the residual effects of a lifetime of separate selfhood continued to operate in this body and mind, but I knew for certain that I was not that, not "me," not the body or mind or the conditioning, not the thoughts or beliefs clustered around that original lie of personal selfhood. So everything started to loosen up. The attachments lost their power. Desires and aversions were not as convincing as they once were. The game continued, but I had left the stadium.

Do you think, then, that this unease you experienced and the vague sense of dissatisfaction that probably everyone experiences is inherent in our lives?

It's inherent in the illusion of duality. Inherent because duality is a lie. We all know on some level that we are pretending to be separate, and we feel it as something missing in our lives. My story could be anyone's story. As a child, I didn't grow up, I grew down. From wide open awareness vast as the cosmos, I shrunk to human size, was caged in a body and taught to confront an "outside" world. No wonder there was unease, and later frustration, and still later a fire that eventually consumed me.

Most people make it through, never seeing the lie as a lie.

Which is how it should be.

But why? It's not real.

Because without the lie of duality, there'd be no world, no game, no dance. And who are we to say that something shouldn't be the way it is? "We" are a figment of our imaginations. Everything should be exactly as it is, not only because it is, but because it's all that is. There's nothing and no one else here to be otherwise!

Still, the burden of having to play the game is enormous.

Yes. It's called suffering, and the great irony is that what we consider to be an independently conscious human being is simply an object appearing in Empty Awareness, and as such is no different and no more "real" than any other appearance. And so the Emptiness, the Subjectivity of the All, is assigned to a mere fragment – not to mention a figment – which then assumes it can do this and that and whatever it chooses on its own, and when things don't go according to plan, suffering ensues. Thus it's man against the world, avoiding what he can't, grabbing all he can before he ages and dies. Having assigned the unlimited role of God to the limited form of "himself," he is doomed to silliness. No matter how wealthy or popular or powerful he becomes, his achievements are, in the grand scheme of things, less noticeable than a grain of sand in the Sahara. What could compare to This, what he *really* is – not *in*, but *as* the grand scheme of things?

So man sets himself up as God, but has only the capacity of one of God's creatures?

Yes.

And you're saying that, in fact, he is God?

Not as man. As man, he cannot say "I am God." That, in the best case scenario, is a recipe for unease, and in the worst, the cause of pogroms and holocausts. He can say, however, "God is I," or "God is no-thing appearing as everything, and I am that." But then of course, it isn't "he" who would say such a thing.

Some prefer to say that one is united with God, a statement which insures God's transcendence and man's relationship with Him.

There is no relationship. There are not two here. There is only unity, and not even that. We use the term "one" merely to point out the fallacy of "two." When What I Am is profoundly seen, "two" become "one," and "one" becomes God "boiling within Himself" (to borrow an expression from Meister Eckhart). God doesn't know what "boiling within Himself" is because he *is* it. Why he appears to Himself from within Himself as Himself is, for Him, not a question. Nor is there an answer. He functions. He manifests.

I've heard you say that God is impersonal, but "boiling within Himself" sounds personal.

It's impersonal in that there is no person here, no entity or self. Once no-self is realized, it – What You Are – is intensely personal. It is true intimacy, in that it never sees other than Itself. It is also familiar. It is recognition of what has always been. I would say it's right in front of your nose, but it's actually much closer than that. It's your very being. You can't *not* be it.

What's the difference between awake and not awake, then?

None, really. It's simply a shift in perception that isn't really a shift, and when it occurs, you realize that this is the way it's always been. Everything is the same, except there's no one here. Everything is the same, except the misunderstanding is gone. That's why you can't attain to it. You already are it. That's why there's no "awakening." No one has ever been asleep. That's why there's laughter. All that's been done in the name of religion: the monuments, the dogma, the ritual, the wars – and for what? For what already is, right here! All I can say is: Look back at what you are looking out of. If you see nothing, believe what you see. If you see it is wide awake and filled with the scene, believe what you see. It's what you are.

ED THE TALKING HORSE

Regarding being aware of awareness, actually seeing aware-
ness – would you say that that's the end, the goal?

No. The end is no-self. As long as there is a sense of self, of
subject here and object there, the end is a zillion miles away.
Only when there is no one, when the only self that can be
claimed is the scene that replaces you, only then is the goal
reached, although the instant it is seen it is also seen that
you were never for a moment shy of the goal.

So there is no journey, and no goal?

Right.

But when I look back and see this awake no-thing, I see I am no
one. It's clearly the case, and it's obviously what I am, so how
can that not be the end?

Looking here at what is looking, there is still a subtle sense
of a looker looking at looking, awareness (subject) aware of
awareness (object). The fact is, looking cannot look at looking, because it's what is looking. Seeing awareness as nothing is not necessarily the same as being no-thing, and even
being no-thing is not the same as not-being-anything – having absolutely no fixed identity – which is closer still to the
truth. I can walk around all day saying "I'm no-thing, I'm nothing," and I might as well be Ed the talking horse, because
I'm still declaring I'm something – in this case a something
called "no-thing." Okay?

Yes.

Well, why the frown?

It's disheartening to think that I'm deceiving myself...but at the same time I have to say that that very thought is only a thought, and when I actually look here, for that split second there are no thoughts, no idea of a "me," nothing but seeing nothing. And I know it's what I am, but it's not like I'm anything!

And is that the goal? Has the goal been reached?

In a way, it has. Right away I return to being a subject here looking at objects there but I really don't believe that set-up anymore. I know it's based on thought, it's a role being played – while here I see undeniably what I really am, which is aware but can't be said to be anything, except maybe the passing show that fills it.

Is it that you want confirmation for what you see? Is this the reason you bring this up? You are the only authority, you know.

Yes, I understand. I am the authority because there is no one else, and no one else here.

And have you noticed that I meet you in that no-place, and not as anyone other than you?

Yes!

Then what am I?

I don't know. Not anything intrinsically real or self-existing. The only thing you can "be" is whatever you are in appearance.

Which is what?

Which is What I am, appearing as "you."

Ah, what a relief! Thank you. For a moment there I thought I was Ed the talking horse!

Smart-ass!

EVERYWHERE, THERE'S MUSIC

I read recently that the body and mind, what I consider my "self," can be thought of as a hollow reed through which the breath of Awareness blows. Another writer compared it to a horn. A horn doesn't know music, doesn't know how to carry a tune, and can't intend to play a song. It's the musician who has the knowledge and the intention.

Yes, it points out the absurdity of our situation, doesn't it? It's like we're applauding the horn and ignoring the musician!

It's the intention part that hits me the hardest. It's almost impossible to believe that I'm not the one willing my actions. And the horn analogy is saying that I'm no more than an instrument, an object, and a hollow one at that!

Well, maybe you *are* willing your actions, and the actions of everything else.

Wait a minute….

Maybe you've downsized yourself, made yourself "human" when you're so much more. When, in fact, you are everything that is.

Which is what the musician is?

Exactly.

Oh! So the intention is still there, but I've mistakenly attributed it to the instrument, to my body and mind. When actually I'm the musician, with all the knowledge and intention in the universe. Wow! That's a stretch!

Yes, the ultimate stretch. But it's closer to the truth. Bodies are merely expressions, are conduits or instruments through which God flows and expresses Himself. Bodies are God appearing as bodies. The same for minds. The awareness you know isn't yours. The human eye doesn't actually see. Seeing is God's business. So once again, it's a case of mistaken identity. Get your identity straight, the boundaries dissolve and the world opens up. This is also why it's said that, upon awakening, nothing changes. It was God the Musician all along, is now, and ever shall be.

But it's a huge change!

Only to the separate self, and the separate self is but an appearance.

You know, hearing this, or should I say, resonating with this, there's a calm that sort of washes over me, a sense of relief. There's really no effort involved in doing what I'm already doing, and there's no striving to be right or perfect because I already am.

Yes, be what you are. But then, how could you not? However, there is a caveat. It is easy after decades of conditioning to carry the sense of separate self into this opening and call it God. The self, when confronted with its demise, can get more than a little sneaky in its quest for survival, disguising itself as whatever it decides to call itself: God, Presence, Absolute Emptiness, etcetera.

But how can I tell if that's happening?

202

If there remains a subtle but noticeable sense of duality, you can bet it's the self, sly old Nick posing as God. If this continues, anything from preacher-ego to severe megalomania is possible. I once dreamed that I was pure consciousness, and all the dream figures were happening inside of me, except they were separate from what I was. The dream realization was accompanied by a feeling of repulsion, a sense that something was dreadfully wrong.

Is there a way out, some sort of reminder? Or will I be blinded by conditioning and never realize it's the ego posing as God?

Well, I suppose it wouldn't hurt to remember that even this posing is ultimately done not by the ego but by God. Better yet, remember that God doesn't *do* anything, He is everything. This knowing, knowing What You Are, is non-dual, and yet the explanation of it is not, obviously because language and thought are necessarily dual. So I'll explain it by saying that God is one-hundred-percent no-thing, and simultaneously one-hundred-percent all that He manifests as, which is everything. Attending to what I see when I look for myself, I see nothing – a no-thing that is awake, boundless, and right here. But I also see that this awake no-thing is filled to capacity with the scene, and filled in such a way that there is no possibility of seeing the two as separate. So you have this Silence, this Stillness, this Awake Never-changing No-thingness, totally at one with this raucous, colorful, ever-changing and on-the-move thingness we call the world. Seen apart, all is seen falsely. Seen whole, all is seen truly. Seen apart, subject and object are assumed. Seen whole, it is the Whole seeing Itself, and there is no separate entity anywhere.

Incidentally, the above explanation, wordy and dual, can be *seen* in a wordless and non-dual flash. I highly recommend it.

You do? And who are you?

Why, you, of course! Who else?

This is either too weird or too wonderful, and I seem to be caught floating in between. How.... How do I once-and-for-all bring this into my life?

You don't. What appears as "your life" is inside of This. And ultimately, the Whole – What You Are – cancels such thoughts about what you can do or can have.

Just that understanding, though – I'm talking about permanently living from that understanding.

What I'm hearing is that you want there to be a separate "you" who has the understanding that there is no separate "you," a separate "you" that permanently lives from that. It's the self saying, "Here, let me handle that understanding that there's no self. I hear it will make me more comfortable and spiritual, and I can always use a little of that!"

. . . .

No comment?

This is so frustrating. Once again you're telling me that there's nothing I can do, and that all of this spiritual trip I've been on is for nothing.

And that's the good news! So relax and be what you are. And why not? You can't be anything else! Just see the striving, the grasping, the wanting to bring the understanding into a so-called "life" – see all of it for what it is. And if you can't, that's fine too. It's all the Musician, playing his tune, and everywhere, there's music.

There's no way out, is there?

No.

And no way to make it better.

No, of course not. It cannot *not* be perfect, so how could it be better?

It seems like every time we have one of these conversations we come to a brick wall, after which everything we say goes in circles.

Shall we stop, then?

Yes. I'm a little upset again.

VANITY

My cellmate is the vainest person I've ever met. Morning and night he's in front of the mirror, primping. He'll spend an hour fooling with his hair, and then after that it's all about getting his pants to sag at just the right height or his cap to sit at just the right angle. I won't even mention the pimples.

I appreciate that.

But really, it's obsessive, and I was hoping you could talk to him.

Me? Why would I do that? He's perfect. He's doing exactly what he's supposed to be doing. If he were to ask for something, I might say yes or I might say no, but obviously he doesn't think he has a problem. It's you who thinks he does.

But it's crazy! How could anyone be that vain?

Maybe he likes what he sees when he looks in the mirror. I like what I see when I look in the mirror, too, The difference is that, to me, it's all a mirror, the entire moment-to-moment changing scene, just as it's presented. I'm totally in love with myself. So, perhaps, is he, except that his love is confined to what appears as a self separate from everything else. The love is there, it's just misdirected. If he were to see through the false self, who knows, he might be Don Juan!

I don't need Don Juan as a cellmate!

No, I suppose you don't.

And it's not that he's in love with himself, it's that he has low self-esteem, so all day long he's trying to fix himself.

Okay, we can go with that story. But I like mine better. Either way, it ultimately translates as love. I'm saying, "This is an incredibly beautiful, fascinating world, and it's all my reflection, it's What I Am, manifesting – it's a love affair between What I Am as No-thing and What I Am as Everything, and they aren't two." He's saying, "I'm so in love with myself, I've got to fix myself so others will love me too." The only difference is a big difference – thinking he's a separate self – but it's nothing more than an innocent lie that he learned as a child. And that's okay, too. It's the way this play, this dance, happens. Or appears to happen. I was lost, and now I'm found, or, I was lost, I'm still lost.

And it's okay to be lost?

Of course. Actually, no one is lost. No one can do it wrong.

So my cellmate is doing fine, all day long staring at a mirror?

Why not? We're all staring at a mirror. And anyway, why do his time? What about yours? Come back and see What You Are, see that he's You, mirroring back what you're mentally projecting. What about the self you are obsessive about, all day long?

Yeah, I guess you're right. It's relentless. I should know better.

No. No need to go there. Somewhere I read that the self is like a supertanker doing 30 knots in open water. The captain cuts the engines, but the momentum of the ship carries it another three miles before it finally comes to a stop. Conditioning can be like that. Even when you cut the engines by seeing What You Are, the supertanker-self keeps lumbering along on sheer momentum.

It's a relief to hear that, because I do this a lot – I complain about others, and when that bubble is burst, I complain about myself. You once told me that there is no difference between others and self, since both are objects in mind. So being down on myself is the same as being down on others, and the fact is, What I Am isn't either. Both are appearances of What I Am, and in that sense are nothing to complain about.

I like that.

But what about humility, then? Most would say it's the opposite of vanity or pride, but it seems more like an absence of self to me.

Yes. True humility is the absence of anyone to be humble. Or to be anything else. It's No-thing recognizing it's No-thing. A genuinely humbling experience is recognizing that you aren't who you think you are. Total humility is God, i.e., Awake Capacity for all that appears, which is anything and everything.

Thanks for your input today.

A pleasure.

HIS HOLY BOOTSTRAPS

You say there is no separation, and yet you talk about Nothing and Everything, which in my mind are opposite poles, the most fundamental separation of all.

No-thing and Everything are not separate. Nor are reality and appearance, absolute and relative, self and other. If I were to say, "Aware Capacity and all-that-it-is-capacity-for," perhaps it would be easier to see?

This isn't to say there is no discriminating within appearance, such as hot and cold, up and down, and so on. If there were no opposites, there'd be no world. However, the appearing relative world is in no way separate from the Absolute. It *is* the Absolute. It is God appearing as a pen, a desk, a thought, a plastic bag, the sky, anger, the television set, dirty socks, a tree, a passing truck, your smiling face – why are you smiling?

Because I just got it, when you said "God." I suddenly saw that all the objects in this room were inside awareness, and that awareness is God. It's all God, isn't it! And it's all right here; it all takes place right here, always.

There is no "elsewhere."

And when you say that all those things are appearance, that doesn't mean they aren't there, it means they aren't separate from God.

They *are* God. That pen, the desk, this room – absolutely everything, the entire universe, is God. Seeing this or not seeing this is in the perceiving. The reality is, there is no dream, no illusion. There never has been. It's only a dream or an illusion when mis-perceived, when seen as a world of separate objects.

Then who is perceiving?

God is! That's the point. All that is, all that could possibly be, is God. God perceives, and perceives only Himself. God is all, and God perceives the all and sees that it is good. There's no "you" here, no "you" anywhere. Never has been, never will be.

It's been God all along?

Yes.

Then…. Then who is it that mis-perceives? Don't tell me….

Yes.

Oh wow!

Is that such a shock? Did you think it was "you" mis-perceiving?

But why? Why would God mis-perceive Himself? Why would He see the world as separate, as not-Him?

I don't know. Ask Him.

I just did.

Ha! So you did. The answer, then, is that God has no idea why. God is, God forgets, God remembers. It's the Sacred Swinging Door, open and closed. It's God's Great Joke, and

He plays it on Himself, and doesn't know why. He doesn't even know why he *is*. Moment by moment He pulls Himself up out of the abyss of nothingness by His own holy bootstraps, and has no idea how he does it! Being, Presence – these are His names, and He rejoices in the wonder of Himself.

You shivered. Are you cold?

No. It's that I wanted it to be me that mis-perceived, and I can't even have that. I can't even be the one who thinks he's separate. I can't even say I'm God, can I?

No. God is no one. God is All That Is, aware of Itself. God is pure unadulterated unadorned Emptiness, wide awake. God is This!

RATIONAL MINDS, DESPERATE SOULS

I can't remember who said it, but there's a saying that goes, "The thinking mind is a perfect servant and a lousy master." I take that to mean that the rational mind, if it thinks it's in charge as a separate self, is the source of much suffering, but if used properly as a tool to transcend itself, it can lead to awakening.

Yes, in a manner of speaking, that's true, although it's important to remember that no one is doing it. The tendency is for the rational mind to claim responsibility, to usurp the sense of "I Am" and declare that it's the one who will transcend itself, which of course only leads to more suffering.

The true source of all "doing" is Impersonal Awareness, felt as "I Am," and the irony, of course, is that Impersonal Awareness is also the source of the illusion of separate self. The rational mind cannot actually transcend itself because it is based on the duality of self and other, but with understanding, it can logically back itself into a corner, saying "not this, not this." And should the illusion of self and other then be abandoned, what remains is This-Which-Has-Always-Been: Impersonal Awareness appearing as Everything. This is why awakening is not attained. It is What You Are to begin with. It is your basic nature, what you have always been and always will be. There is nothing else!

The use of zen koans would be an example of backing the rational mind into a corner?

Yes. Self-inquiry can do the same, as can any *via negativa*, as well as a journey into the rational limits of modern science. From the point of view of this rational mind, however, the most strikingly persuasive method is a matter of actually looking to *see* one's absence. It doesn't get any more convincing than that.

Looking at the Emptiness you are looking out of?

Yes.

For me, the problem with that is that the rational mind says it's too simple. It can't be this easy. It can't be right here. It can't be the real or the great "Emptiness" of Buddhism. It's just a piece of it or an example of it.

Tricky, that rational mind.

You think that's what's happening? Rational mind is trying to talk me out of it?

As it will with any method, when backed into a corner. It either pretends not to notice or tries to forget. Or it cranks up the logic machine and declares war against whatever threatens it.

It's almost too direct, this looking and seeing.

I agree. It puts off most of the "seeker" crowd, the new-agers and anyone whose self isn't ready to give in to no-self. Of those who look, only a few will actually believe what they see. The rational mind can be relentless with excuses, and may pull out all the stops before it gives up its precious self. So you get this see-saw battle of seeing and forgetting, or seeing and calling it something else, something logical and personal. Still, looking and seeing is the fast track to Here, and if all is ready, it's over.

What do you mean, over? The separate self will be gone?

213

No, the self will still be there, it simply won't be central anymore. It won't be seen as existing in its own right. Like everything else, it will be seen as a part of the world "out there," an appearance. It continues to do its thing as a member of an infinite web of interconnected and interdependent possibilities collapsing into manifestation, and in this role, it is one-hundred-percent necessary to the Whole.

But not real in the sense that it's permanent, that it's Who I Really Am?

Right. Only this Emptiness, this Clarity, this Awake Shining Presence can be said to be real, and it isn't anything at all. Amazing, no?

More than amazing. Shocking, when you look, and the excuses stop.

And something you said earlier – about it being a "piece" or an "example" of Emptiness but not the real deal or complete package – is another of those popular excuses.

Yes, it's saying that I'm over here and you're over there and we each have our separate consciousness, which is the usual way of looking at oneself and the world.

Exactly. When you look, what you see is what you are, and it's complete, just as presented. No-thing here, filled with everything – which is the whole of it, as it is, no matter what appears as "everything." Truly seeing this, you are no longer "you," no longer a "self." Seer and seen dissolve into Seeing.

And attachments and longings disappear?

They may continue, but they're seen as irrelevant. They may

hang around for awhile as part of the conditioning of the body and mind, of the illusory self, but when seen as having no importance, they may wither and die. The point is, it no longer matters if they are there or not there because, like everything else, it is all This: Impersonal Awareness manifesting.

What about renunciation as a spiritual technique? I'm thinking of Saint John of the Cross and Theresa of Avila who severely deprived themselves in order to know God. Or those who retreat into caves in the Himalayas, foregoing all contact with the outside world and living for decades in extreme conditions, with no medical care, barely eating, not even lying down to sleep.

You mean, is it necessary in order to awaken? Absolutely not. If it's in the cards for you to awaken, you'll do so. Even if lying in bed watching television and stuffing your face full of nachos!

Sounds like my kind of practice!

Suffering can be beneficial in that it has a tendency to kick one in the existential pants. Especially when it takes the form of desperation, of extreme depression.

The "dark night of the soul."

Yes. Some say that the dark night of the soul is a prerequisite, but that's not true. There are no prerequisites for being what you already are.

Yes, but for ending the illusion? Couldn't desperation be a prerequisite for that? Most of the awakened that I've read about have gone through some form of personal hell.

No. There are no prerequisites. Some have experienced desperation, others longing, while still others were in the midst of ordinary living. The play of separation ends when it ends.

So I needn't work myself up into a state of desperation. Is that what you're saying?

Oh I'd like to see that! You at the end of your rope!

It could happen. You've said it yourself – anything can happen in the realm of appearances.

Yes, but I meant on this planet!

THE TEN-GALLON HAT

You hear a lot these days about mankind being on the verge of reaching a higher plane of consciousness, which will be our next great evolutionary phase. I've been thinking about this, and I've got to say that, given the current conditions on the planet – nuclear threat, global warming, disease, etcetera – the possibility of extinction is very real, so that a new phase of consciousness based on the perennial wisdom may be the only thing that saves us.

That's a nice story. It's got Hollywood potential: drama, purpose, the possibility of a happy ending. I like the time-is-running-out scenario: Just when we're about to exterminate ourselves and end all planetary life, on the brink of total disaster, up pops our superhero "mankind" wielding a new and higher plane of consciousness – call it "enlightenment" – so that, just in time, all are saved from the evil forces of endarkenment. Praise God in Heaven!

You're being sarcastic again.

Yes, it's a habit, I'm afraid.

Okay, fire away!

It's very simple. I look here. I see no-thing, pure Emptiness. It's wide awake, and it's obviously what I am. It never changes. It can't change because there's nothing here *to* change. Evolution, on the other hand, is all about change, and as such, is about as real as the ten-gallon hat I'm wearing.

You're not wearing a ten-gallon hat.

Thank you.

So evolution is an appearance.

Yes. It's a concept to explain change in individuals and groups of individuals over a period of time, all very "scientific" and "factual" in the world of appearance, but of absolutely no consequence to What You Are, which was never born, never dies, and never changes. Everything that changes does so *within* What You Are. All of time and space are within What You Are.

Yes, but if everybody sees this, or if at least a large percentage of the population does, wouldn't that make a difference?

There *is* no "everybody." There is only Pure Empty Awareness, always awake, always here, always now – so much here and now that "here" and "now" have no meaning. It is already perfect, already done. Nothing can touch it.

Okay…. I'm caught in the dream, but I'm trying to understand this. Let me ask you something else, then. At the last Buddhist meeting the teacher talked about the various awakened gurus in our particular lineage, and all of the incredible powers they had. And then he started talking about what it's like to be in the presence of someone who is awake, the aura of love and compassion they exude, how others are drawn to them as if by a magnetic force. And for some reason, I got irritated and depressed listening to that – like awakening is so remote it'll never happen to me, like it's reserved only for the select few, the yogis who read minds and levitate and all that. Was he right, and is it a lost cause for someone like me?

You know the answer to that.

Yes, I guess I do, but maybe I need to hear it from you. He even asked if anyone in the group had ever been in the presence of an awakened being and felt the power, the vibe. Of course, we all said no.

So what's the answer?

That there's no such thing as an awakened being?

Yes. "Awakened" and "being" are mutually exclusive, and can never relate.

But what about the powers? Do true gurus have powers and give off auras you can feel?

In the dream, do certain gurus give off auras? Do some read minds, attract crowds, convene with animals, melt snow with their naked butts? Probably. Do others trade stocks, drive trucks, sell lingerie, write romance novels, farm cranberries, go entirely unnoticed? Probably. Some have powers and give off auras; others have car payments and give nothing to no one. The point is, who gives a damn? Who is there to care about any of this? Seekers get hooked on powers and auras, as if somehow this defines a guru's authenticity or level of enlightenment. A true guru will be the first to tell you that such things have nothing to do with enlightenment. One guru meditates all day, so his followers meditate. Another guru smokes and drinks, so his followers do likewise. A third guru likes to walk in the garden, so all his followers find a garden they can walk in. It's crazy.

So there's nothing special about a guru?

No. Once again: There is no such thing as an awakened being.

It makes no sense, though, because awakening is such a huge, momentous event.

It is not a huge momentous event. It is not even an event. Events are experiences; events happen to individuals. With awakening, nothing happens. The reason nothing happens is because the dream is seen as a dream – as not real. Awakening is the end of what wasn't there to begin with.

The end of the story?

The end of everything you ever thought was anything. And we can also say that the evolution of the universe – which is everything – is God's return to Himself. From the Beginning it's been His story, and all that ever was, is, or will be is a manifestation of and by Himself, returning to Himself. And it all leads to this index finger – His finger—pointing at the Luminous Awake Nothing that He is. And in that final single act, there is recognition. What You Are, both transcendent and immanent, is Him.

SCAM ARTIST

Are you enlightened?

No. Are you?

No.

Ain't life grand!

I guess so. But I thought you were....

No.

Then what are you?

I don't know.

I'm talking about the person standing in front of me who talks about awakening.

Oh, him. He's a scam artist. Not a very good one, but he tries.

Tries to scam us? You've been playing us all this time?

You bet. Anything to take you out of your game. Here, standing in front of you , is a sham, a fraud. Fakery is his *modus operandi.* Watch out, because his play is to steal everything you think you are, and he doesn't know why.

Well.... What can I say? I thought you were the real thing.

No, no. I have never been any sort of thing.

So you've been pretending?

Pretending to be me? Yes. Please, take "me" with a grain of salt. There is nothing serious here, nothing important in these clothes. "Me" is the great pretender. Don't believe a word he says.

Well...listen, I've got to go. I'll see you later, then.

Yes. Thank you for stopping by.

NON-DUALITY PRESS

If you enjoyed this book, you might be interested in these related titles published by Non-Duality Press:

The Light That I Am, J.C.Amberchele
Awake in the Heartland, Joan Tollifson
Painting the Sidewalk with Water, Joan Tollifson
Only That, Kalyani Lawry
The Wonder of Being, Jeff Foster
An Extraordinary Absence, Jeff Foster
Awakening to the Dream, Leo Hartong
From Self to Self, Leo Hartong
Dismantling the Fantasy, Darryl Bailey
Standing as Awareness, Greg Goode
The Transparency of Things, Rupert Spira
Ordinary Freedom, Jon Bernie
I Hope You Die Soon, Richard Sylvester
The Book of No One, Richard Sylvester
Be Who You Are, Jean Klein
Who Am I?, Jean Klein
I Am, Jean Klein
The Book of Listening, Jean Klein
Spiritual Discourses of Shri Atmananda (3 vols.)
Nobody Home, Jan Kersschot
This is Always Enough, John Astin
Oneness, John Greven
What's Wrong with Right Now?, Sailor Bob Adamson
Presence-Awareness, Sailor Bob Adamson
You Are No Thing, Randall Friend
Already Awake, Nathan Gill
Being: The Bottom Line, Nathan Gill

For a complete list of books, CDs and DVDs, please visit:
www.non-dualitypress.com

Forthcoming books from NON-DUALITY PRESS
2011

THE ULTIMATE TWIST *by* Suzanne Foxton
A novella: addiction, love, therapy and awakening

THE TELLING STONES *by* Riktam Barry
Enlightenment, the spirit of the '60's and modern times

GONER *by* Louis Brawley
The last five years with UG Krishnamurti

ESSENCE REVISITED *by* Darryl Bailey
Slipping past the shadows of illusion

THE LOVING AWARENESS IN WHICH ALL ARISES
by Rick Linchitz
Dialogues on awakening

BLESSED DISILLUSIONMENT *by* Morgan Caraway
Seeing Through Ideas of Self

THE LAST HUSTLE *by* Kenny Johnson
Finding true happiness and freedom in prison

THE PLEASANTRIES OF KRISHNAMURPHY
by Gabriel Rosenstock
Revelations from an Irish ashram

DRINK TEA, EAT CAKE *by* Richard Sylvester
Dialogues and observations of a tour in Germany

CONSCIOUS.TV

9 780956 643247